The FAMILY FRYING PAN

Bryce Courtenay was born in South Africa but came to Australia in
1958. He applied for and was granted Australian citizenship six
months later and celebrated by marrying Benita that same year.
She blessed him with three sons. In 1995 he was awarded the AM in
the Order of Australia. He lives in Sydney.

The Family Frying Pan is his tribute to his adopted country,
which since the 1950s has opened its gates to welcome five and a
half million migrants, many of whom came to Australia to escape
the hunters and to build a better and safer future for their children.

Also by Bryce Courtenay

The Power of One

Tandia

April Fool's Day

A Recipe for Dreaming

The Potato Factory

BRYCE COURTENAY

The Family

Frying

Pan

Illustrated by Ann Williams

William Heinemann Australia

Published 1997 by William Heinemann Australia
a part of Reed Books Australia
35 Cotham Road, Kew 3101
a division of Reed International Books Australia Pty Limited

Designed by Ann Williams and David Rosemeyer
Typeset in Garamond and Bodega by J&M Typesetting
Printed and bound in Australia by Southbank Book

National Library of Australia
   cataloguing-in-publication data:
   Courtenay, Bryce, 1933– .
   The family frying pan.
   ISBN 0 85561 699 7
   I. Williams, Ann, 1942– .
   II. Title.
A823.3

WRITERS' BLOC

THE READER IS ALWAYS RIGHT

To my two sons Brett and Adam
who would not be who they are if their
great-great-grandmother had not walked
across Russia carrying a large cast-iron
frying pan.

'Don't forget to thank the blue cat'

When I was very little and about to go somewhere on my own, my mother would instruct me, 'Don't forget to thank the blue cat!' Which was her way of saying I should thank everyone. And so I thank all those who helped me with this book, the numerous generous friends, other writers from whom I borrowed facts and received assistance, and all the people who inevitably help to make a work of fiction. But always there are those who must be singled out for praise: my wife Benita who reads everything first. Annie Williams who shares this book with me and whose lovely paintings and drawings bring life and joy to my words. Belinda Byrne and Meredith Rose, my editors. Essie Moses for her help in matters Jewish. Kath Davies, Maria Dickson, June Lotzof, Mike Lotzof and Barbara Goldin who supplied the delicious recipes, and, finally, Lisa Lintner who tested them and then tested them again until they were perfect. (If you mess them up it is entirely your own fault.) I thank you and I thank the blue cat.

Contents

The
Family
Frying
Pan

My name is Sam, well Samantha really, but it's always been Sam, chopped to one syllable. I have a brother, Samuel, who's two years younger than me and a major pain.

Samuel is one of those kids who knows everything and has this seriously scientific mind, his brain is like a train tunnel and goes straight for the light, straight down the line, never diverging.

It was him who told me that the first atom that ever existed still exists in every living thing on earth. The first atom to come into existence is living in me. Hea...vy! So you see, you couldn't call a fifteen-year-old extreme like him anything but Samuel, even though cutting *his* name down to Sam would make a lot more sense than chopping down mine.

I think my being called Sam comes from the expression, 'Oh, Sam!' – like that, with an exclamation mark. Which is what my family have been saying ever since I can remember. The kids at school say it, my teachers say it and sooner or later everyone says it after I bring out one of my great thoughts or theories.

My theories about things may not be very scientific but that doesn't mean they couldn't happen. People nod their heads when wonder-brother explains something, as if they're amazed at his genius brain. But when I come up with a great thought all I get for it is, 'Oh, Sam!' Which you can say in about a hundred different ways, all of them not very complimentary.

I often find that I can get some great thoughts and theories kicking around in my head when I'm walking home from school after Sue, my best friend, has peeled off to her house which is two blocks from me. It's then that I have some prime thinking time.

Sue's really upset at the moment because her mum thinks her dad has been seeing this other woman and they could be splitting. Getting a divorce. She's *really* mixed up because she likes them both. Her dad isn't a creep or anything. Her mum hasn't looked after herself and is a bit overweight and uncool. Personal appearances shouldn't be important in sustaining a marriage anyway.

Sue can see why her dad could do it, and she's all mixed up because she can take her mum's side too.

Mixed up is supposed to be normal when you're teenaged, whatever 'normal' means. Young people are supposed to be in a continual state of confusion, if you believe magazines like *Dolly* and *Cleo* which are full of stuff about changing relationships, teenage sex, surging hormones and image, but mostly uncertainty about the future.

So when Sue left, it got me thinking about the issue of being mixed up beyond just the physical and emotional stuff and problems in families which nearly everyone's got. I thought about the mixed up blood in our veins. It's quite interesting. I could have bits of Cleopatra or Martin Luther King or Einstein floating about in me, though Einstein's bits are probably in Samuel. It really could be true if you went back far enough, which is as far as I'd got in my thought processes by the time I reached the back gate of our house.

I burst into the kitchen and dumped my bag on the floor.

'I'm starving,' I announced.

'Pick up your bag before someone trips over it.'

'In a minute. I'll just –'

'Now, please!'

'Yes, Mum.' I hauled the bag onto a chair and reached for the cookie jar.

'Do you realise that I am the sum total of every human ever

born on this planet?' I said through a mouthful of choc-chip cookie. 'Mixed blood, we've all got it.'

Mum looked confused, but then she often does when we try to have a meaningful conversation. I waited for her to say, 'Oh, Sam!' but she didn't, her mind was on other things, like cooking.

'Forget mixed blood and help me by mixing up a batch of scones.'

'Dungeons and Dragons night, right?'

'Now, Sam! It's only once a month,' she scolded me.

My brother had this smart pack over once a month to play Dungeons and Dragons, a sort of super brain game left over from kindergarten. The scones were for them, though they'd probably have preferred pizzas from Pizza Pete's.

'Yeah, right.'

I finished chewing and rinsed my hands and rummaged around and found the ingredients. I'd make date scones, they liked them best. I took all the stuff over to the opposite side of the kitchen table to Mum and started mixing flour into a bowl.

I thought of Sue who has this theory that you should never learn to do anything around the house like learning to cook, but if you're forced to, you do it so badly that your mum gives up on you. If she knew I was baking a batch of scones for my brother she'd seriously think about ending our friendship. She'd say he should bake his own.

'Not so much butter,' said Mum.

'I'm not!'

'Just follow the recipe!' She pointed to my end of the table.

I looked. She'd put a recipe book down opened to 'scones'. I can bake scones standing on my head. Date, raisin, even pumpkin scones, I've done it dozens, probably hundreds of times.

But my mum, who is an expert cook, can't make anything without the recipe book open in front of her. She never looks at it, it's just there sort of as part of the ingredients. She's making a bread and butter pudding and she's got Margaret Fulton's recipe book open. She's been making bread and butter pudding for my dad at least once a week practically forever and could do it blindfolded and in her sleep. Arguing against my mum is like swimming across Bass Strait to Tasmania against the tide, which got me thinking again.

'Mum?'

'What?'

'You know those Huon pines they chopped down in Tasmania when they dammed the Franklin River? Just think, some of them were saplings more than a thousand years ago!'

'How do you know?' she said, sort of semi-interested.

'Growth rings! Some old trees showed growth rings of nearly two thousand years on them. Mum, we could be like that, kind of like a family tree, each generation a new ring so that we end up being a bit of everybody.'

Mum rolled her eyes towards the ceiling. I could see what she was thinking. Why did she have to give birth to a daughter with such a weird brain. When I was in Year Ten one of my report cards said, 'Samantha is a good lateral thinker.' I think Mum thought it meant 'latrine thinker' because I was always reading on the toilet. Latrine is the word my dad uses for the toilet.

'Oh, Sam!' she said dismissively and got up and went to the fridge for the milk.

But I liked the thought of human tree rings and pounded the dough in my excitement.

Mum turned from the fridge. 'A light hand for scones, Sam.'

'Yeah, right.'

I glanced down at the dough and my eye caught the left-hand page of the recipe book Mum had opened for me. I knew the book well, it was one my mum had inherited from my gran, who probably inherited it from her mum, because it was truly ancient. On the left-hand page in old-fashioned printing were the words: 'When he comes a-courting, scones are always a favourite!' The words were framed in a circle of roses with four ribbons attached sort of floating off, one into each of the corners which were occupied by a fat cupid with a drawn bow. The ends of the ribbons were twirled conveniently to hide their private parts.

'Are all cupids male?' I asked Mum.

My mum sighed. 'What are you talking about now, Sam?'

She tucked a strand of her reddish hair behind one ear. I suppose she's gone a bit pudgy like Sue's mum, too, though my dad doesn't seem to mind. I turned the recipe book to face her and pushed it closer to her end of the table, with a doughy finger pointing to one of the cupids. She put her head to one side and looked at the picture.

'Are all cupids male?' I asked again.

'I think so.' She seemed a bit uncertain. 'Anyway, the males are always the ones with the arrows. They're the hunters.'

Which got me thinking yet again. At school this man from UNICEF gave us a lecture. He said there are four hundred wars going on in the world today, mostly about ethnic differences, mainly with people who live in the same country but with different religious or ethnic backgrounds. The hunters are still out there. But their bows have turned into missiles that blow up whole villages. He said these wars are really against helpless women and children who always end up suffering the most. I think there's also a hidden political agenda in most of those wars. Men who want personal power and use religion and colour or racial differences as the excuse. Women and children don't go to war because their neighbour is a different religion, do they?

Last night on the news, after they'd shown the IRA blowing up the citizens of London, they switched to Grozny in Chechnya, where the Russians were killing people who, about five minutes before, were also supposed to be Russians.

They showed this very old lady who had whiskers sticking out of her chin alone in a room where the windows had all blown out. She was crouched over a small spirit stove. On the stove, which had one little blue flame licking up, was this huge cast-iron frying pan. In the frying pan was a potato and an onion, which was all she had left to eat. Everyone she knew was dead or had fled, and she was completely alone in the world. All she had left was her big black frying pan.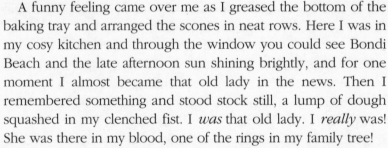

A funny feeling came over me as I greased the bottom of the baking tray and arranged the scones in neat rows. Here I was in my cosy kitchen and through the window you could see Bondi Beach and the late afternoon sun shining brightly, and for one moment I almost became that old lady in the news. Then I remembered something and stood stock still, a lump of dough squashed in my clenched fist. I *was* that old lady. I *really* was! She was there in my blood, one of the rings in my family tree!

I dropped the dough and went over to the cupboard under the stove and pulled out this old cast-iron frying pan, the Family Frying Pan. You have to say it like that, all in capital letters, because the Family Frying Pan is the very same frying pan my great-grandmother carried on her back as she walked across Russia to escape the pogroms.

Pogroms were the raids on the Jewish people by the Cossacks who would ride into a Jewish village and kill any Jew they could find. In the Russia of the Tsars, Jews were open season all the time. Two Cossacks would each grab a little baby by the feet, mount their horses and swing the babies round and round as though they were clubs. They would charge towards each other from opposite directions, each trying to knock the baby out of the other's grasp. If the two baby heads connected there were cheers all round.

My great-grandmother's village was raided by the Cossacks and everyone in it, except her, was killed. She'd seen the Cossacks coming when she was working in a cornfield late in the afternoon and had no time to run and warn the villagers. Terrified, she watched helpless as she saw the synagogue go up in flames and then at last the Cossacks ride away.

Her own parents had been killed in just such a raid when she'd been ten years old and she had been brought up by the rabbi's family, where she had been treated more or less as an unpaid servant. At that moment, watching the small synagogue burning, she decided to walk out of Russia in search of a world where men didn't kill babies and 'Jew' wasn't a dirty word. What a hopeless hope that turned out to be!

She stayed all night hidden in the cornfield and in the early morning of the next day she crept into the silent village. Not a single villager remained alive. The Cossacks had dragged all the villagers from their homes and slaughtered them in the square outside the synagogue. There was no time for her to grieve, the Russian peasants would soon come to ransack the dead village and if they found her she would be killed. Besides, there was no one in the village she could truly say had loved her or had been especially kind to her.

It was already late autumn and she didn't have a warm coat and her shoes were worn. So, she found Mrs Abrahams, whom she knew as a member of the women's congregation. Mrs Abrahams, who always considered herself a little better than most, owned a good pair of boots made by the village bootmaker for Passover.

'Mrs Abrahams, this is Sarah Moses,' she said politely to the dead woman. 'God will help me to walk to freedom in your nice new shoes, and I thank you for your generosity. May you dance in Heaven wearing a pair of golden slippers.'

Then she looked around for the best coat she could find on a dead villager. 'God will keep me warm, Mrs Solomon, but He needs a helping hand

13

from you. A final act of charity from someone who was never very famous for her charitable works. When you arrive in paradise, may you wear a cloak of peacock feathers that falls all the way from your shoulders to the ground.'

With Mrs Abrahams' boots on her feet and Mrs Solomon's coat on her back she prayed and said thank you to God. 'Lord, with the help of Abraham the Patriarch to guide my feet and the wisdom to wear a warm coat that comes from Solomon, maybe I've got a good chance to make it out of here.'

Then she turned to the dead Mrs Solomon. 'I'm sorry, my dear, but there are not ten good male Jews left to say the Kaddish for you and also that nice Mrs Abrahams. When I get out of Russia, I promise I will pay a rabbi to say the prayer for

the dead in the village with a special extra mention for the two of you.'

After making this promise, my great-grandmother looked among the smouldering ashes of the rabbi's home until she came upon a very large cast-iron frying pan in which she had cooked a

thousand meals for his family. 'I swear to God that the generations to come who eat from this pan will taste no more of the bitter fruit of life,' she vowed, lifting the frying pan from the rubble.

My great-grandma died before I was born so I couldn't ask her the obvious question: why a frying pan? I can hardly lift it when I hold it by the handle. She had a whole village of dead people's things to choose from and yet she took a dumb old frying pan. It was so heavy that when she slung it on her back she had to balance on one spot before she could get the necessary momentum to move.

I must explain. The frying pan has a hole in the end of the handle. She threaded a piece of rope through the hole and looped it and then hung it backwards around her neck. She was as straight as a pencil when she walked.

She was only a very small person, so it was a pretty stubby pencil. When she died at eighty-seven, my dad says, she still stood straight as a barrack-room guard. The silver scar where the rope from the frying pan had rubbed her thin little neck in the walk across Russia was still plainly visible.

I should mention here that the adventures of my great-grandmother and the Family Frying Pan have all come down to me second- and third-hand and the scar tissue around her neck may be a bit of an exaggeration. But in the pictures

I've seen of her she's always wearing a blouse with a lace collar pulled up high under her chin. So maybe not.

'Some day, someone in the family will write a book about your great-grand-mother,' my mother sometimes says. 'If they do, they must call it *The Family Frying Pan*.'

It seems that Russia was coming out of a very severe winter that year. (I think it always is, isn't it?) People were starving all over the place and the roads were filled with people trying to find a better place to live, not only Jews, but other people trying for a new life. Each night they stopped at the roadside in small huddles and my great-grandma, who had spent the day looking for twigs and pieces of wood as she walked along, would light a fire and place her frying pan on the flames.

'Gather around, friends!' she would shout at all and sundry. 'I have a good fire here and a fine frying pan, God will supply the rest!'

I mean, it stands to reason she must have gone hungry some nights, but that's definitely not how the story goes. The story has it that someone would reach into the interior of a shabby coat and produce an onion. Somebody else would find a potato concealed in the pocket of a pair of threadbare trousers, a few cabbage leaves would emerge from inside the blouse of one of the women, then a bit of pork fat from another's bag.

Pork fat! What am I saying? Not pork fat! That would be anti-Jewish and she probably wouldn't have accepted it. Though I'm not so sure. If I was starving I'd ask God to forgive me and pretend it was chicken fat.

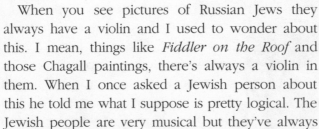

The point I'm making is that the frying pan was always filled with a little bit from here and a little bit from there. My great-grandma would cook whatever there was and then divide it carefully among everyone in her huddle. The Family Frying Pan, with a little help from God, never failed her. A hot meal was enjoyed by all and then someone would bring out a violin and they'd sing some of the old melancholy songs about

Mother Russia and cry a bit and tell stories with sad endings.

When you see pictures of Russian Jews they always have a violin and I used to wonder about this. I mean, things like *Fiddler on the Roof* and those Chagall paintings, there's always a violin in them. When I once asked a Jewish person about this he told me what I suppose is pretty logical. The Jewish people are very musical but they've always had to flee from something or someone and just as often they are in a tearing hurry. It's the middle of the night, they can't exactly take the piano, but the violin is portable and can always earn someone a meal, even if it's played on a street corner. 'That's why today there are more Jewish violinists in the world's great symphony orchestras than any other people,' he said.

Well, it seems my great-grandma got quite a long way on her frying pan. But somewhere along the way, at the end of a day's long journey, the Family Frying Pan sitting on the embers wait-

ing to do its daily chore, the soldiers of the Tsar attacked the refugees.

Spring had come at last and though it was still cold, it wasn't freezing. My great-grandma had taken off Mrs Solomon's coat and wrapped it around a baby who had been born to one of the women in the group two months before. She placed the baby carefully beside the fire.

The soldiers, all on horseback, came charging in, striking at people with their swords and these big clubs they used to smash heads as they galloped past. People were running everywhere and screaming and my great-grandmother turned to see the troopers charging towards her with their swords held high.

Well, she wasn't going to leave the baby or the coat, and certainly not the frying pan. She grabbed it and slung it by its

rope into its accustomed place about her neck where it rested face down against her back. She was so panic-stricken she didn't feel the hot pan burning through her jumper, searing the flesh on her back. She threw on Mrs Solomon's coat, grabbed the baby and ran.

By now she was well behind the rest of the fleeing people, some of whom had reached the safety of the nearby woods. Others lay dead where they'd been stabbed or clubbed down, blood and brains splattered in the mud.

A captain, wearing a high-plumed helmet and gold epaulettes on his grey coat, galloped furiously up to my great-grandmother and stabbed her in the back as he dashed past. The sword snapped instantly and the impact flung him out of the saddle and under the hooves of the oncoming horses.

My great-grandmother was sent flying but somehow she managed to hold onto the baby as they rolled together in the mud. She got to her feet to run but a second horseman swung at her with his mighty club and sent her careening again. The blow from the club would have killed her instantly, for it was aimed at the centre of her back and would have snapped her spinal cord.

But in the yelling and galloping and screaming no one heard the clang as the club struck the solid metal of the frying pan, and the trooper let out a cry of anguish as his wrist snapped and the club fell to the ground.

Screaming in terror (also unheard in the general noise), my great-grandma again rose to her knees just as a third horseman struck at her with his sword. Again the blade snapped and the rider was unhorsed to land head first on the frozen ground, breaking his neck instantly.

He must have been the last of the troopers because my great-grandmother, still clinging to the baby, managed at last to get to her feet and stagger to the safety of the woods. From where they hid among the trees, the others who had escaped witnessed the whole thing and immediately declared it a genuine miracle, and my great-grandma a living saint.

They had seen two great swords snap like matchsticks as they tried to pierce her body, and had also witnessed the terrible club strike and bounce off her harmlessly. Moreover, she had held onto the baby throughout the ordeal. They concluded that she had been sent by God to deliver them safely out of Russia, and they marvelled that her surname was Moses, the very same as the great Jewish leader who had led the children of Israel out of the land of Egypt.

Their faith in her was not misplaced. Twenty people made it safely out of Mother Russia led by Mrs Moses, a little Jewish lady who walked straight as a pencil.

Eventually my great-grandmother made her way to Australia, which she claimed was the only nation where she felt completely safe. Everyone in the whole world had come here and mixed their blood in one glorious big mix-up, so nobody was much interested in being a hunter. After all, heaps of Australians either started out being prisoners of the hunters, or came here to escape them. Of course, when she came here, the Family Frying Pan came with her.

I have just worked out how the world works. It has nothing to do with the colour of your skin or the slant of your eyes or the God to whom you pray, but only whether you are a hunter or a gatherer. The hunters destroy, they are the killers and the rapists. The gatherers love, nourish and share, they are the peacemakers. Blessed are the peacemakers.

As I sit here at my bedroom window watching the sun set over the ocean in a perfectly calm, beautiful, high-blue-sky sort of Australian day, I think of that old lady in her small room in Grozny in Chechnya. The city is burning around her and she is holding the handle of a cast-iron frying pan over a tiny licking blue flame with only an onion and a potato to eat. I know that she is in my blood, that she and her frying pan are a part of my family history, of every family history, a part of me, of all of us. I've been there before, we all have, at some time in our bloodline's past.

You see, we have to care, we have to stop the hunters. If we are to be saved we must become gatherers. If we stop caring about that old lady in Grozny we stop caring about ourselves and we all die a horrible, empty, lonely death and the hunters win all over again! Not caring is called compassion fatigue; you see so much blood and stuff on television and videos and at the movies that you don't think it's real any more. But it is when it's on the news and if you ignore it, think about it as being someone else somewhere else, then you're allowing them to murder someone's great-grandmother of the future. If the Cossacks had got my great-grandmother I would never have happened. It's a sobering thought because *you* may not have happened either.

My wish for the world I live in is that we put an end to hunting and killing and all become gatherers. As my own

nanna, who first told me the story of her mother, Mrs Moses, and the Family Frying Pan, once said, 'Remember always, child, the *pan* is mightier than the sword.'

That's not true, she didn't say that at all! I just made it up this very moment. That's why my mum still rolls her eyes and says with a sigh, 'Oh, Sam!'

Next Year in Jerusalem

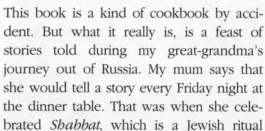

This book is a kind of cookbook by accident. But what it really is, is a feast of stories told during my great-grandma's journey out of Russia. My mum says that she would tell a story every Friday night at the dinner table. That was when she celebrated *Shabbat*, which is a Jewish ritual which happens every Friday night when they light candles and say a special prayer about delivering the Jews out of bondage. The last words are a wish they say when they drink the Passover wine, a sort of toast: 'Next year in Jerusalem.'

It's a pretty weird thing to hope for, if you ask me, seeing the mess things are in in Israel at the moment, with too many hunters and not enough gatherers walking about the place.

The reason my great-grandma told a story on Friday nights was because she said *Shabbat* was her story, when she was delivered out of the bondage of the Tsar and his bloodthirsty Cossacks and found her way to Sydney. Australia isn't exactly Israel, but it's a lot less troublesome, if you want my honest opinion.

Now, before the stories begin, I have to tell you about the seasons. You see, the little band of misfits travelled through Russia for more than a year. To understand what they went through you have to be familiar with the seasons, because it's not like Australia where the weather stays more or less the same the whole year around. I want you to be able to imagine for yourself what it was like living outside, exposed to the elements. Also, at the end of each story there is a recipe. I absolutely guarantee the recipes will work, my mum's cooked them and she's a terriffic cook. But also, they came out of my great-grandmother's cookbook and are in her own handwriting and you couldn't imagine someone who could lead a group of people single-handedly out of Russia being careless with a recipe, could you?

The stories are in my great-grandmother's voice. My grandpa recorded all the stories after the war. My mum says the old *buba* had a beautiful way of telling stories and they always began with the time of the year, because my great-grandmother said that the blood in our bodies worked to the rhythm of the tides and the phases of the moon and the changing of the seasons, and some recipes work better at different times of the year. I suppose a little like hot cross buns at Easter and plum pudding at Christmas, which of course doesn't work all that well in Australia so we justify it by calling it tradition. Traditions are important, don't you think? They tell us who we are and where we've been and they are part of the human tree rings we inherit to tell us we are not alone.

SPRING

It has been a lovely spring day, still cold, for the ground has not fully thawed, though the sun is bright enough for hope to leap like skipping children into our hearts. The streams in the woods, muddy pools in the late summer, now rush with the blue melt of snow and, even though the ground clanks like iron when you stamp your foot, stiff green shoots of daffodil and lily of the valley push through the frozen mud. The sap rises in the forest so that the branches, the small tender branches, show tight green pods at every extremity. High in the sky a lark sings and the breeze carries the first scent of honey-suckle and almond blossom.

Summer

It is the sunsets, always the sunsets that make me feel that the day on the road has been worthwhile. That the dust and the flies, brown puddles and turgid rivers and the heat are bearable as we walk our road to freedom. Russia is such a big country, an endless place where walking all day seems to bring you to the same spot. And everywhere the struggle is to stay alive, so much space filled with so much pain. But it is easier to find food in the summer,

when the gold of the ripened cornfields stretches so far across the horizon that its reflection burnishes the sky. Summer evenings are an enchantment, that part of the day when Mother Russia rests her burden for a few short minutes to paint the sky with the burning colours of hope.

Autumn

The autumn days are beautiful, mellow and tranquil at first. There is a ripeness about everything, a proper conclusion to all things. The sky is a serene blue and there is a feeling of restfulness in all of us.

But then the days start to brood, at first a little sulky, or in polite language, a trifle melancholy, as the light begins to fade and the days to shorten. Finally impatient and spent of energy by the long hot summer, the mood darkens and a sense of malevolence, of unease, thickens the air.

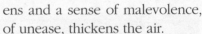

The wheat and the corn are harvested, the fields shorn, scythed clean and exhausted. The sky now glows the colour of old pewter and the leaves, the tears of the dying forest, begin to drop silently to the ground. The wind now comes from the north like a shrill whistle through clenched teeth. A fine rain falls. Misted spray that seeps into our clothes and squelches in our boots. The sun is now pale as if seen through turgid green water and the air is stale and still. Darkness comes suddenly, like the snap of a malevolent finger.

WINTER

God has gone absent from Russia, left us to fend for ourselves, defeated by the endless snow, the malice of the howling wind, the remorseless ice drifts, the bone-white horizon bleak beneath the firmament where the stars have gone out in a vacant sky that offers no hope.

We plod on when we can, stiff legs wrapped in rags, but for the most part there is no winter journey in this ghostly landscape. We have stored what little food we have against these evil, endless months, we are rats gnawing on anything we can find. The old people die and our tears freeze against our cheeks. Death is such a constant visitor that we can only sigh, it is a mouth less to fill and the threads taken from old backs can now be used to cover younger, stronger bones. Winter in Russia is the white wolf of suffering and each day we dread its howl and fear that it will run us down, that it will tear and devour us, so that we will not make it to the end of this stark and terrible bleakness.

Evening, Somewhere in Russia

We have all of us gathered what twigs we could find on the day's journey and made the evening fire. Now it has burned down to the embers. My famous Cossack-defying frying pan,

with a dob of lard, sits sputtering and spitting on the soft glow. The meal, as usual, will be turnips, potatoes and onions. And maybe, if we are lucky, a little red cabbage, all of which are scavenged by my fellow travellers and

given willingly at the day's end to be shared among us. Occasionally, a scrawny old winter-worn rooster is bargained from a peasant for a kopek or two, or a nest of field mice or a clutch of quail eggs discovered. These are happily dumped into the pan. But mostly it is the same: turnips, onions, potatoes, beets and perhaps a little cabbage thrown in for good fortune, and with it what's left of the rough, coarse ember bread we bake at dawn for the day's travelling.

Mr Mendelsohn has stopped playing his violin and we all sit quietly for a few moments.

'What shall we have tonight?' I ask my fellow travellers. 'What delicious concoction, splendid banquet or magical meal? What delectable and memorable supper, special treat or delight to assault the nostrils, to send our taste buds into a frenzy and to seduce our palates?'

And always someone will raise a hand. Whether it is a learned professor or a musician, a chef's wife or a blacksmith, a scholar, or circus acrobat, it doesn't much matter. In the business of food there is no pecking order for all come equally to the table of the imagination.

'Ah!' someone will say. 'How well I remember dining with the Tsar, His Imperial Majesty himself. And, of course, the Tsarina and the five girls and Prince

Alexei, the heir to the throne. Let me hasten to add, this was not a State occasion, only a simple meal with a few close friends in a smaller ballroom in the grand palace in St Petersburg, no more than two thousand present. Such a cosy little feast.'

'The story! The recipe!' we will all urge at once. 'Tell us what we will be tasting tonight!'

And so the recipe-storyteller will begin and we experience the delicious salivation of anticipation. The contents of the pan, now bubbling on the fire, will soon be ready. We will share the food, the turnips and potatoes and onions and cabbage, perhaps only a few spoonfuls each. But, ah, what spoonfuls! For we feast on the words of the storyteller and if words can make a stomach contented, by journey's end we will all be plump as partridges.

Such a Clever Little Mushroom

ANYA PUTS UP HER HAND TONIGHT. SHE IS A THIN woman with a sad face, perhaps in her late twenties or younger, it is hard to tell. Russia and a poor marriage make short work of a beautiful bride. Yet there is still something there. Her eyes are blue as cornflowers and there is a fullness to her lips and, surprisingly, none of her teeth are missing. They are white and perfect, so that her smile is serene and angelic. At night she will sing to the children with a voice like a thrush and she loves to read aloud. It is as if her books are good friends which she must share with us, for Anya has love to give to all. Her baby is the infant I scooped up when the soldiers of the Tsar attacked. Anya is in love with Mr Mendelsohn, the violinist, and their love, even out of wedlock, is pure and clean and beautiful. Often she will gather wild herbs and mushrooms in the fields and woods and add them to our humble evening fare to make a feast out of a turnip, or turn a potato into a prince of vegetables.

'I shall tell you of my wedding feast so that we may choose a dish to eat tonight, a soup to serve to a prince,' Anya says as we sit watching the Family Frying Pan bubbling on the fire.

She sighs and begins her story.

I was chosen to be the bride of the landowner's only son, a peasant girl to compensate for a bloodline that had lost its vigour. My husband-to-be was a poor specimen, with eyes too close and hairy brows that joined across the bridge of his nose. He was rich and needed a male heir, and I was strong and, I suppose, pretty enough. Besides, it was an honour my father, who was a poor man, could not afford to turn down. So, for a good horse and a small cornfield, I was sold to the landowner's son.

As for myself, I was given no choice in the matter. Love was not a word used easily in our village and the honour and good fortune bestowed on me was thought by all to be very great. The old women would cackle in my ear, 'He is ugly, Anya, but think nothing of it. In the dark between the sheets, who is to tell pretty from ugly? Give him a male heir and one to spare and you can grow fat and live in comfort for the rest of your life.'

The wedding day came and the fat priest joined us together in a chorus of hymns and vows and prayers to bless our union with male offspring. Then we sat together at the wedding feast, my husband and I, while the village danced and feasted in our honour and we had nothing to say to each other.

The silence built like an abyss between us as the dancers whirled and the village men got drunk on good vodka. The fiddlers played love songs and the old women ogled the ugly groom and smacked their toothless gums at the thought of the splendid wedding cake to come. Some begged me to sing but the laughter and the song had gone out of me.

'Why did you marry me?' I asked my husband at last, my heart thumping like a Tartar's drum at the boldness of my presumption.

'You have broad hips and big tits,' he snorted. 'There will be milk in your breasts for the male children you will give me. I have seen you carry a burden worthy of a mule, and I am told you can cook to delight a man's stomach. I desire no more from a woman, save silence and obedience.'

'But I can read to you,' I cried. 'I alone among the village girls can read and I also know a little Latin and the new science of botany!'

'I have no time to listen, nor you to pleasure yourself with books of which we shall have none in my house.'

'Then shall I sing to enchant you?'

'It is enough that the birds sing when they steal my corn. What will you steal from me when you sing?'

'Shall I play the harp then?' I asked him. 'The harp to rest your soul when you are weary.'

'Vodka will do that task well enough, the harp is for idle fingers and your hands will not be idle for any waking moment of the day. You will rise at the cock's crow and you will be last to bed.'

'What then, my husband? How then shall I please you?'

'You will cook and clean and fetch and carry and remain silent and breed my many male children and feed them on your paps until they are three years old. If you do all of these things well you will not be beaten more often than is good for you.'

'What shall I cook to please you most?' I asked trembling.

'There is a chicken soup my mother makes as thick as a plate of stew and seasoned with fresh herbs from the fields and wild mushrooms from the forest. It is the aromatic herbs that make the difference. Do you know these herbs, woman? Can you make this soup?'

'Every village girl knows them. The soup, too; I shall make it for you, but not as well, I daresay, as your sainted mother.'

'You will make this chicken soup for me every night and serve it silently and with humility. If it is not as good as the soup my mother makes you will be beaten, for my mother says it is this soup of herbs and wild mushrooms and plump chicken meat that gave my father the vitality and vigour to conceive a son as splendid as myself!'

And so I made the soup a thousand times, each time more delicious than the last. The years rolled by and the landowner died and now I must call my husband 'lord'. Each night he sniffed at the soup. 'Not the right smell!' he yelled. 'A scrawny chicken no less!' Then, after wolfing down the bowl of soup, he would beat me. 'Not as good as my mother made!' he shouted as he knocked me down. 'It is the herbs! You have the herbs in the wrong proportion.' He pointed to my flat belly. 'You eat my bread and, see, you remain barren, you are cheating me of sons, of male offspring, you are nothing but a miserable village whore!'

Then one night he sniffed imperiously at the bowl and I waited for his admonishment, but he said nothing. When he had slurped his soup like a pig at a trough and wiped his mouth with the back of his hand he looked at me, his beetle brows dark and twitching, his small eyes black and hard as agate. 'Perfect! The aroma perfect, the chicken perfect, the herbs in all the right proportions! Tonight, woman, you will conceive me my first son!'

That night as he mounted me he was taken quite suddenly with a great gnawing pain in his belly and was soon overcome with a terrible vomiting sickness. 'You have poisoned me with my mother's chicken soup and what's more you have failed to give me a son. I have no heirs, my good name is lost forever,' he screamed between the sharp spasms of pain.

'No, my lord, the soup is good,' I protested. 'It is your mother's soup, made just the way you like it, perhaps a pinch more salt, nothing else.'

'Call the physician, woman!' he groaned.

The doctor came in his top hat and fancy horse and buggy and shook his head. 'Call the priest!' he shouted.

The fat priest came and prepared the sacrament and heard my lord's final confession and then gave him the last rites. I stood behind the priest so that I might hear my husband's words of regret, the sins committed and the absolution so generously given.

'Forgive me Father, for I have sinned,' my husband moaned. 'I have sometimes beaten my mule too hard and I have not always given a full measure of corn to those who till my fields!'

'God is merciful, my son,' the priest intoned. 'The pain in your stomach is sufficient penance. Besides, a mule has no soul and is a stubborn creature at the best of times and is known to try the patience of a saint.' The priest licked his thick lips. 'As for the peasants, it is their lot in life to be cheated by the landowner.' He made the sign of the cross. 'You could this very night enter the gates of paradise, my son.' The priest paused, coughed and then continued. 'This I can guarantee if you leave a little thought for God's kingdom on earth. The church coffers are empty and we need a gold cross set with precious stones, rubies and diamonds and pearls from the Caspian Sea. A cross so that all who come to pray for redemption will know we are a parish of the utmost importance in the eyes of Heaven itself.'

'I am poisoned, I shall die!' my husband screamed again and pointed a trembling finger at me. 'She, this witch, has poisoned me, she must be made to rot in hell, you must name her a mother of Beelzebub!' His fingers clawed at his fat, hairy stomach and the blood ran from the corners of his mouth. But the man of God seemed not to hear. With the doctor there as witness, he was writing out a contract, his quill scratching out a last will and testament. In his mind he could see the afternoon sun streaming through the stained-glass windows of the church to reach the golden crucifix set with gems blazing with the passion of Jesus, our Christ Lord.

It was the midnight hour and the silver moon peeping through the window was as large as a late-summer melon when at last the priest held the paper out to be signed. Groaning, my stricken husband, absolved of his earthly sins and about to enter the gates of paradise, reached weakly for the pen. But before he could hold it in his trembling fingers he was suddenly recovered. The pain which a moment before tore him apart was now quite gone, plucked like a mouse from a tussock of grass by the sharp talons of a hawk. What was about to enter the gates of Heaven was back on the road of life again.

'A miracle!' the priest exclaimed, clapping his fat hands together. 'Sign here on the dotted line! God, in his infinite mercy, has spared your life! You must repay Him at once!'

'Ah! Not so fast!' my lord said, shaking his finger at the priest. 'If God had needed my money for a golden cross He would have allowed me to recover *after* I had signed your paper!' He grinned, his small eyes mean and cunning, and I could see he was very pleased with himself. Then, with a backwards wave of his hand, he dismissed the holy father. 'Go now, priest, I shall send you six bags of corn for the poor.' He pointed to the door. 'Go, go, or will you stay to witness how I beat my perfidious wife for her bad cooking?'

And so the priest departed in the moonlight, cursing and shaking his fist in a most ungodly manner, and my lord beat me until I was black and blue and finally fainted.

And then on the dawn of the fourth day after his miraculous recovery, when all around had seen his usual bad temper and witnessed his health completely returned, my lord rose from his bed as the cock crowed in the yard and loudly called for borscht, sweet tea and cinnamon rolls. But before a morsel had touched his lips, he fell to the floor at my feet and all this was witnessed by three farm workers who had brought in the milk for churning. He tried to rise, but his body was strangely paralysed. The three men carried him into his bed, their eyes as big as the bottom of a vodka glass.

The men responded to my tearful pleas to call the doctor and left in haste to do my bidding, leaving me alone in the bedchamber with my husband.

'I blame you, witch!' he croaked, but he could say no more. His tongue now lolled, swollen and useless, from the corner of his mouth.

'Ah!' I said, now quite calm, so that I spoke in a most respectful whisper. 'Lord, do not blame me, blame the songs that have not been sung, and the music that has not been played and the stories in wise books that have not been read beside the firelight. Blame the herbs from the fields, the secret herbs that can keep a girl barren if she chooses. Did your sainted mother not tell you of these? Finally, blame the wild mushrooms from the forest that make such a delicious soup, all the safe and the dangerous members of the fungi family. Let me tell you about them, the good ones and the bad.

'The tiny red mushroom with white dots you see in all the fairy tale books, *Amanita muscaria* – did I not once tell you I knew a little of Latin and botany? It is what the shamans of the Koryk tribe in Siberia call the *wapag*, which is the name they have given to the tiny tribe of fairies and goblins, elves and pixies which inhabit the land of mushrooms and toadstools. The Koryk use the *wapag* to cast magical spells which alter the mind, to see things that are not meant to be observed, devils and demons and other phantasmagorical hallucinations.

'Then there is the Liberty Cap, *Psilocybe semilanceata*. It too produces a state where dreams mix with reality and it is popular among the more educated priests and much used by them to frighten and then to trick gullible nobility into making donations to the Church.

'There is also the Poison Chalice, *Entoloma sinuatum*, very toxic, but often mistaken for a common edible field mushroom. But not by me, my lord, for I have fed you none of these; only the good and the beautiful have gone into your chicken soup.

'Ink Caps to bring a flavour of nuts. The giant puff-ball, sweet and delicate. *Aminita caesarea*, Caesar's Favourite, the most delicious of all, usually found under beech trees, a subtle and sublime mushroom that turns a competent soup into a triumph of the soup-maker's art. All of these and more I found and prepared lovingly for you, and my best efforts were met with a scowl, a pig's grunt and, often enough, a severe beating.

'Now let me tell you about my little treasure, *Amanita phalloides*, the Death Cap, a fungus usually found under an oak tree. It has a sweet smell, though a little too sweet if you ask me, not unlike lamb's urine. And what a lovely deception it carries, for it has a pleasant nutty flavour, or so it is said; I have not myself tasted it. But, of course, you would know its flavour, you two are by now four days acquainted. Did you not compliment me on my chicken soup just four nights ago? The famous chicken soup that was to bring you a son and heir? It was the very first compliment you have paid me and so I am not likely to forget it, or *Amanita phalloides* which allowed me to please my husband just once in my entire married life. It was a soup, you said, just like your mother used to make and you called for a second helping.

'And now there is perhaps just sufficient time for me to explain to you just how this pretty little fungus works. First it makes you sick so that for six hours you vomit all the good food you have stuffed into your fat gut until there is only green bile and pain. Pain so great that you beg God to let you die. And then, six hours later, a miracle! A cure sufficient to give you the strength to beat your wife mercilessly. Then, three days pass, the mule is beaten again, the corn measured short, and normal life resumes. And, along with them, any suspicion of foul play, so that all swear to your robust good health and give praise to

God for a miracle to be credited to their own church, performed by their own holy Father Markovitch.

'Then comes death, silent as a cat's footfall. This time there is no mistake and the prince of darkness comes too quickly for the doctor in his horse and fancy buggy, or the priest in his dirty cassock with white spittle at the corners of his mouth, his wine and host bread in a box under his arm along with paper, ink and pen. This time, my dear husband, there is time only for these few words of comfort from your loving wife.'

I bent over him and with the ball of my thumb closed his staring, lifeless eyes, and then I went to find two kopeks to place upon the lids.

'Such a clever little mushroom,' I sighed.

1 × 1.5 kg/3 lb chicken, all skin and visible fat removed

2 cloves garlic, roughly chopped

1 large onion, roughly chopped

2 large carrots, roughly chopped

2 stalks celery, roughly chopped

1 bay leaf

6 whole black peppercorns

3 parsley stalks, crushed

6 large field mushrooms, thinly sliced

2 tablespoons/30 g/ 1 oz butter

2 tablespoons cornflour, mixed with a little cold water

salt and black pepper, freshly ground

¼ cup/75 ml/2½ fl oz double cream

4 sprigs parsley, chopped

FOREST and FARMYARD BROTH

METHOD

Add the chicken, breast-side up, garlic, onion, carrots, celery, bay leaf, peppercorns and parsley stalks to a large, heavy-based saucepan and pour in enough water to cover.

Bring the saucepan to the boil, reduce the heat and simmer gently, partly covered, for 1 to 1½ hours until the chicken meat falls off the bone.

Pour the chicken and vegetables through a colander, reserving the stock. Remove chicken meat from the carcase and chop. Set aside.

Place the strained stock in the refrigerator to cool and allow the fat to set on the surface. Skim off the fat and place the clarified stock in a large saucepan.

Sauté the sliced mushrooms in the butter and set aside. Add the cornflour to the stock, bring up to a gentle simmer and stir until thickened. Season with salt and freshly ground black pepper.

Add the chopped chicken, mushrooms and cream, simmer for a further 2 minutes and serve garnished with chopped parsley.

Serves 6 to 8

The
Feast
of
PEARLS

It is Mr Mendelsohn who has volunteered to

tell a story tonight. We are all surprised, for he is a man of few words and what little conversation he has beyond politeness is reserved for Anya, the pretty mother of his infant son.

We do not miss his conversation, because his violin speaks for him with an eloquence that no human tongue could possibly emulate. Each night at the fireside, after we have 'feasted', we are transported away from Russia, from tyranny, hunger and despair, to a land conjured from his fingers and his bow. A land where children play without glancing over their shoulders and men are not slaves to a harsh landowner but find regular work for decent wages, and their women till the fields and keep enough of what they grow to feed their families.

We all watch a little warily as Mr Mendelsohn puts away his violin. Such a careful man, he lays it neatly into its scuffed and scruffy case, as though laying to rest a much loved friend within the faded velvet lining. For a moment we see his long fingers caress the brilliant lacquered instrument and then the lid comes down like a coffin and snaps shut. Such an unprepossessing case to house so eloquent an instrument. The violin, which has come to be a living part of our journey, a part of the glow of the firelight and our sweet rest from the weary day, will be silent tonight.

Mr Mendelsohn coughs nervously into his fist. 'I shall tell you of the Feast of Pearls,' he says. He coughs again and looks up at the stars as though he is remembering.

'I once lived for a short time in a fishing village on the shores of the Black Sea where palm trees grow and the flowers of the tropics bloom and yellow butterflies as big as your hand flutter against a cloudless sky.'

'Here in Russia? Palm trees, tropical flowers, blue skies, butter-flies? Surely you are misinformed,' cries Professor Slotinowitz, who, by the way, is not only a refugee from The Academy of Science in Moscow but also from the imagination. A man who thinks only in facts and what he calls logical deduction.

'Perhaps I have not got the words?' Mr Mendelsohn says, uncertain.

'No, no!' we all yell. And I say quickly, 'The words you've got are already perfect! Such lovely words, tropical and butterfly words, and words warmed by the sun; continue if you please, Mr Mendelsohn!' We all glare at the Professor of Know-everything, without any imagination to save his soul.

Mr Mendelsohn still looks confused. 'I know I am not good with words,' he stammers and his eyes go to the violin case and his voice grows uncertain. 'I can play this place for you. I will let my violin tell you of the evening breeze like rushing waves through the palm trees and the splash of colour made by the butterflies in the shining midday air. With my bow I can paint the brash colours of the tropical blooms and the slap and shush of warm waves that spill onto foamy silver beaches in the moonlight.' He reaches eagerly for his violin case.

But Anya places her hand upon his elbow. 'Your words are like jewels in the sun, my lover,' she says quietly. 'You must continue.'

Anya seems to give Mr Mendelsohn fresh courage and he starts to speak again.

'In this village on the shores of the Black Sea the fisher-folk push their boats out to sea when the stars are still bright in the firmament and dawn lies quietly asleep beyond the horizon. They fish all through the heat of the long day, and in the evening as the sun is setting they return with their small boats filled to the gunnels and glinting with the minted silver of fish.'

'What kind of fish?' Professor Slotinowitz demands to know.

'Shhh!' we all chorus, a rudeness for which we must be forgiven because the professor is such a know-all sort of a person that sometimes, in the name of good manners, we are forced to be rude to him. Only Olga Zorbatov is his equal in the clumsy-remarks department, and you'll hear some more about her later.

Mr Mendelsohn blushes. 'Alas, I must beg your pardon, Professor, I know nothing of the kinds of fish and cannot tell a sardine from a cod.'

'Fish will do nicely, Mr Mendelsohn,' I say and then turn to the professor and address him quite sharply. 'Thank you very much, Professor Sloti-know-all-o-witz, the fish mentioned in Mr Mendelsohn's story have gills and tails and silver scales and that is quite enough to know about them!' I turn back and nod to Mr Mendelsohn to continue.

'Well, one day, not long after first sunlight, when the boats had been out no more than two hours, they were seen returning to shore. The women mending nets, baking bread and tending to their children came running down to the water's edge to see whatever could have happened to bring their menfolk home so soon.

'They watched as all the small boats converged on one boat and the men jumped out into the shallow waves. They were lifting something from that one boat. The men were crowded around the burden as though anxious to share in the pride and glory of their catch. They waded up onto the wet sand and then they parted to show four men carrying a mermaid. Her silver tail was flapping in great agitation, changing colour with every twitch so that the women were forced to shade their eyes from the furious flashing brilliance. The expression on the mermaid's face showed clearly that she was unafraid but not in the least pleased, and the sounds she made were not unlike the mewing of a newborn kitten, not at all elegant and contrasting badly with her astonishing beauty.

'Now everyone knows what a mermaid looks like, but few people have actually been close enough to one to see what a truly beautiful creature she is. This mermaid had perfectly scalloped scales that changed to every colour in the spectrum at her slightest move, and which ranged in size from that of a large silver coin at her waist to less than a small child's pinkie nail where her tail fanned out.

'The skin above her waist appeared completely human, unblemished and as soft to the touch as the ermine lining of the Tsar's coronation crown. Around her neck she wore a perfect string of blue pearls. Her hair hung in swirls to her shoulders, dark as midnight, and framed a milk-white oval face. Her eyes of luminous green shone with the fire of cut emeralds. Where it might be supposed her nose would be petite, with perhaps the slightest upturn to compliment such a sublime face, it was nothing of the sort. In fact, it was imperious, a trifle too large, a commanding nose, a nose for a princess destined to be a queen. Her lips were generous and shaped like a cupid's bow and the glimpse of her teeth allowed by her angry mewing suggested they were as perfect as South Sea pearls.'

Mr Mendelsohn clears his throat. 'There remains only the delicate matter of ...' He begins to blush furiously, clearing his throat again and then coughing into his fist. Then he looks over at Anya for help. When he sees she is feeding his baby son, the infant's tiny greedy mouth sucking and smacking on her wet nipple which only just protrudes from her blouse, he seems to take courage. 'Her, er ... breasts!' His voice is hardly above a whisper. 'They were perfectly shaped cones of sheer delight, rounded like the crescent moon, and each crowned with a small rosebud.'

'Tush! Mammeries and nipples!' the professor snorts. 'There isn't the least thing romantic about such female appendages! Cows have them in any number, sows too, cats and dogs and stoats and weasels! Udders give me the shudders and tits give me the ...' He pauses, looking mischievous. 'Well, anyway, it rhymes!' He points to the little violinist. 'You play a commendable violin, Mendelsohn, but you tell a most improbable tale.' He rises slowly and, leaning on his walking stick, he starts to walk from the fire then pauses and turns back. 'If it were my story and I were you, Mendelsohn, I'd slice your mermaid neatly in half, make a damned good fish pie out of the bottom half and use the top half as the prow of a sailing ship, which I'd sail straight over the horizon all the way to America!'

The professor glares at me for a moment, daring me to reprove him. 'No offence, Mrs Moses, but we need schemers not dreamers to get us out of this mess. The murder story Anya told last night was exactly what we needed to whet the appetite. A nice bit of chicken soup revenge to lighten the burden of our journey out of Russia. To use a fishy metaphor, I would rather go hungry tonight than listen a moment longer to this load of codswallop! Good night to you all.' Then he stomped off, snorting like a rhinoceros, into the night.

I must say it took a lot of encouragement to get Mr Mendelsohn back to his story. And to tell the truth, we were to regret our efforts, for once he got started it was much of the same again. The artist in Mr Mendelsohn forbade him to miss a single detail. The colours and shapes of the clothes on the washing line of a house they passed carrying the mewing mermaid back to the village, a fish hawk eyeing them balefully from the top of a tree, a brief dog fight, two black and red beetles mating on a tropical leaf. And so much more, until the turnips, potatoes and cabbage in the Family Frying Pan were overcooked and still we hadn't come to the Feast of Pearls. It was going to be a long, long night and I could see everyone was beginning to envy the professor's decision to go to bed, even though they would miss the evening meal in the process.

I proposed that we stop to eat and then allow Mr Mendelsohn to continue. Who was to know that a man who spoke so seldom had all those words in a great reservoir inside his head? But they were there all right, a lifetime of unspoken observations which now bubbled over the dam wall in his brain and caused a verbal flood that overwhelmed us all. By the time he had completed his story all but Anya and myself had long since fallen asleep beside the fire.

For the sake of a neat ending I will try to tell you the rest of the story as quickly as possible. The mermaid proved to be not such a good idea after all. For a start the village possessed only the *mikvah* bathtub, that is the bath used by the women for ritual cleansing when their time of the month came, and she took possession of it. Moreover she had the most enormous appetite and consumed a large portion of the fish brought in every night. Her mewing never seemed to stop except when she sang.

Now, if you believe in the legend that mermaids lure lonely sailors to their doom on the rocks with their beautiful singing, forget already that theory. According to Mr Mendelsohn, the opposite is true, the sound is so raucous that the sailors fleeing with their hands over their ears are unable to steer the boat which then crashes willy-nilly onto the nearest available rocks.

Well, to cut a long story short, the men in the village soon saw their families going hungry and, of course, they decided to throw the mermaid back into the sea. But that's where the trouble started. Happily housed in the village *mikvah*, fed like a queen every day, the mermaid had no intention of leaving. So when the men came to take her back to the sea she let out a single high-pitched sound that popped the eardrums of the six fishermen allocated the task. This caused great consternation in the village until someone pointed out that now six good men were permanently deaf they could transport the mermaid back to the ocean without fear. But when they entered the small room where the bathtub stood the mermaid flashed her emerald eyes, and the rays coming from them were so fierce that the six fishermen were instantly blinded.

In desperation the villagers decided to starve the mermaid, but soon after she'd missed her first meal she began to sing. The sound was so awful that small children started to vomit, dogs went crazy chasing their own tails and yowling pitifully, and men and women buried their heads in the soft sand or dived underwater, so that they might experience a few moments' relief. They soon capitulated and gave the mermaid an entire day's catch.

This was the state of affairs when, one evening, Mr Mendelsohn found himself tuning his violin under the window where the mermaid was housed.

Now, you will agree that the tuning of a violin can be a most unpleasant experience for the human ear, but not so, it turned out, to the ear of a mermaid. After a few moments of catgut scraping the mermaid's face appeared at the window, and it was obvious she greatly liked what she heard.

Mr Mendelsohn, seeing her pleasure, played a few perfect notes on the violin, whereupon the mermaid's emerald eyes grew dark and her expression displeased.

So Mr Mendelsohn followed with a few strokes of the bow that sounded like a rooftop caterwauling and, at once, the mermaid clapped her hands in glee. Using every discordant note he could summon, the little violinist set to playing and the mermaid began to splash and cavort in the *mikvah* tub until she couldn't contain her pleasure a moment longer. She leapt from the bathtub out of the window to pirouette; her wonderful fishy tail flashed and gyrated as she danced in a frenzy of delight to the terrible screeching and scraping of the violin.

Instantly Mr Mendelsohn made for the shoreline with the mermaid dancing behind him. When he reached the water's edge he continued until only his shoulders and the violin were free of the waves and the mermaid, as though in a trance, followed him.

She began to swim in a circle around him, sometimes rising out of the water and leaping joyously in an arch over his head. It was plain to see that she had fallen hopelessly in love. Suddenly she stopped, took the string of pearls from about her neck and placed them over Mr Mendelsohn's head, and then she kissed him.

It was a kiss so sweet that Mr Mendelsohn, transported, forgot to make the terrible rasping sounds and started to play a Brahms violin concerto. The mermaid was so horrified by this sublime music that she covered her pretty ears and dived deep down into the waves and was never seen again.

I looked at Mr Mendelsohn and shook my head. It was late and I would need to be up at dawn to bake bread for the next day's journey. 'So tell me, Mr Mendelsohn, I do not wish to be nosy but you have straw stuffed in your boots, half a dozen patches in your britches and your elbows stick out of your overcoat – what happened to the mermaid's pearls?' I admit it was a bit forward, some might even say rude, but I was too weary to mind my manners.

Anya opened her blouse and there, draped about her neck, was a magnificent double string of pearls which glowed in the moonlight. 'There are ninety-nine only,' Mr Mendelsohn explained. 'One pearl I took and sold so that the village could buy new fishing nets and a boat with a donkey engine and have a great feast, the Feast of Pearls, to celebrate the departure of the mermaid.'

'So, you are a rich man already, Mr Mendelsohn? Tell me, please, why do you travel with us? You could take a train and travel first class and eat three meals a day and smoke a Cuban cigar, and be out of Russia in three weeks, never mind nobody!'

Mr Mendelsohn sighed. 'The pearls were a gift to me by the mermaid but the authorities soon heard about the perfect set of blue pearls and claimed that, because they came from the sea, they rightly belonged to the Tsar and that I had stolen them. I do not care for money, Mrs Moses, only music and love and a desire for freedom. I have been branded a thief and will be sent to Siberia if I am caught, so I am forced to flee in the most inconspicuous manner possible. To take a train or the steamboat would mean certain capture but no one will think to look for me in such a dispossessed little group. Now I have two of my desires.' He glanced lovingly at Anya and the baby and picked up his violin case. 'I have love and music and soon we will all be free. When we get out of Russia, Anya and the baby and I will go to America and there I will sell the pearls and buy the Boston Symphony Orchestra where I shall take up a position as First Violin until the day I die.'

Magnificent MERMAID PIE

3 medium carrots, peeled and finely sliced

½ bunch spring onions, chopped

2 small, very ripe tomatoes, chopped

3 stalks celery, including tops, chopped

3 cloves garlic, chopped

2 bay leaves

1 kg/2 lb firm white fish fillets, cut into 2.5 cm/1 in pieces

225 g/8 oz scallops, washed and trimmed

225 g/8 oz green prawns, shelled and deveined

1 tablespoon fresh parsley or basil, finely chopped

salt and black pepper, freshly ground

4 sheets puff pastry

a little milk

WHITE SAUCE

2 tablespoons/30 g/1 oz butter

2 tablespoons plain flour

1½ cups/375 ml/12 fl oz milk

2 tablespoons parmesan cheese, finely grated

½ cup/125 ml/4 fl oz dry white wine

salt and black pepper, freshly ground

METHOD

To make the white sauce, melt the butter in a saucepan. Add the flour and stir to combine. Cook gently, stirring, for 2 minutes. Remove from the heat, cool, and add the milk, stirring until smooth. Add the cheese, wine and season with salt and pepper. Place over a gentle heat and cook, while stirring, for 5 minutes until smooth and thick. Set aside to cool.

Set up a steamer over rapid boiling water and steam the carrots, spring onions, tomatoes, celery, garlic and bay leaves for 10 minutes. Add the fish, and steam for another 5 minutes. Add the scallops and prawns, and steam for a further 2 minutes. Remove the bay leaves.

Preheat the oven to 180°C/350°F/gas mark 4. Line a 23 × 35 cm/ 9 × 14 in pie dish with two sheets of pastry and push together to seal the join at the bottom. Trim off any excess pastry and prick the base with a fork. Bake for 10 minutes in the preheated oven and allow to cool to room temperature.

Spoon in the seafood and vegetable mixture, and sprinkle with the parsley or basil. Pour the white sauce over and cover with the remaining sheets of pastry. Trim and prick the pastry top, and lightly baste with milk.

Increase the oven temperature to 200°C/400°F/gas mark 6 and bake for 15 minutes or until the top is golden brown. Serve immediately.

Serves 6

The Princess Tatiana and the Indian Myna Bird

PROFESSOR SLOTINOWITZ IS UP EARLY AND COMES

upon me just as I am laying the second batch of small wheat loaves into the frying pan to bake. Five loaves already lie on their backs to cool on a small muslin cloth. We will eat them during the day's journey and, together with our evening meal, it is just sufficient to keep us from starvation. As for the rest, we hope always to come across a patch of wild berries, or an apple orchard with fruit on the ground from an overnight windfall.

It is surprising what may be scavenged in a summer and autumn landscape. Locusts have a nutty taste but can only be eaten when the bitter-tasting head and the papery wings are removed. A clutch of birds' eggs eaten raw is a gourmet discovery, and fat grubs that live under the bark of fallen oaks and elms, birch and lime trees are also delicious. The acorns we gather we grind for coffee and they can be eaten raw when there is nothing else. Roasted chestnuts are a forest delicacy, and all make life possible in the summer and autumn, but spring, with all its bright promise, yields very little to the hungry gatherer. Winter brings us nothing but the bitter cold.

'Good morning, Professor,' I call, not stopping to shake his hand, as my own is floury from kneading the bread dough.

'Humph!' he replies, clearing his throat. Then he adds without a great deal of conviction, 'I apologise, Mrs Moses.'

'Whatever for?' I ask.

'Last night, that stupid story, I could not contain myself.'

'Not so stupid, as it turns out,' I say mysteriously, 'but very interesting, Professor. You should have stayed for the end.'

'Impossible! It is dreamers who have ruined my life. Impossible, ridiculous, impractical, stupid, irresponsible, selfish and thoughtless dreamers!' He pauses and sniffs. 'The bread smells good!'

I cut a warm loaf in the centre and hand him one half. 'It's not extra, Professor, that is your ration for the day.' I point to the kettle bubbling on the fire. 'There is coffee made from ground acorns. You have your own cup, yes?'

The professor takes his bread and coffee and sits on a fallen log. Then he reaches inside his coat and produces a knife and fork. A red bandanna also appears and he fluffs it in the air before arranging it neatly on his lap. Placing the small half-loaf on the cloth he commences to cut it into tiny squares and eat it as though it were a meal of sausage and potatoes. His manners are correct and come from the city and he sits with a straight back as he chews each tiny square thoughtfully, as if it were the afore-mentioned sausages, or even the most delicate cut of beef or some other exquisite morsel.

When the meal is completed I watch from the corner of my eye as he upturns the crumbs from the cloth on his lap into his cupped hand. Then he moves a small distance from the fire, where he stands with his hand held out high above his head. It is still very early and the air is misty blue and not yet sharpened by sunlight and the professor's breath is smoky as he stands perfectly still, a tall man with a pointed beard and glasses, every inch the mathematical genius, very much the great scholar.

I continue to work, watching the bread and the coffee kettle and feeding twigs to the fire. I have half a mind to reprove him, even the smallest crumbs are treasures when you are hungry, and here is the professor holding the crumbs in the air and offering them to the wind as though he is carrying out some religious benediction.

He is also making a soft, breathy whistling sound which could be a prayer, though I would never have thought him to be the praying type. So it is with some amazement that I see the first small bird alight on his hand and then, in a few moments, half a dozen more flutter down out of a clear blue sky and come to rest on his now overcrowded palm. They begin immediately to chirp and quarrel amongst themselves as they compete for his delicious offering.

It takes the birds no time at all to polish off the crumbs and so I wait for the professor's next trick. These are not very substantial birds but every little bit makes a difference and the professor is, to say the least, a pretty poor scavenger and makes almost no contribution to our larder.

The birds are now hopping on the old man's shoulders and his head and all he has to do is pick them off one at a time, squeeze their heads between his thumb and forefinger and drop them into his pocket. Today such a cruel thought would not occur to me, but I have a full belly and a warm bed to go to. Starvation is not a condition which encourages sentimentality.

But the professor does no such thing and as each of the tiny creatures hops onto his hand he kisses the downy feathers and lifts them into the air to send them on their way. Soon all the birds are gone and the professor dusts his hands and strolls away as though nothing very unusual has occurred.

The next batch of bread is now ready and I shake my head. How can someone be so smart and also so stupid? In the case of the professor of know-everything, a bird in the hand is just as useless as two in the bush. I sigh. There will be no flavour of meat in tonight's offering.

I had almost forgotten the incident with the birds when some weeks later the professor put up his hand to tell a story so that we might choose the dish our evening meal would become that night.

That he should volunteer a story comes as a complete surprise. On most nights his attitude towards our stories is dismissive, though with only the slightest encouragement he will expound one of his theories or explain how a steam train works or an iron boat floats on water. He is not so much a storyteller as a fact teller and seems totally uninterested in food.

As a matter of fact, the professor is the only one among us who appears perfectly content with the food I serve straight from the Family Frying Pan. Turnips, potatoes and cabbage are for him an elegant sufficiency.

So when Professor Slotinowitz volunteers to tell us a story we don't quite know what to expect. Another of his endless theories perhaps? Or, at best, a hasty, tasteless meal cooked in a laboratory on a Bunsen burner while some pointless experiment occupies his mind which, when solved, will not put an extra crumb on his family table. That is, of course, if the professor ever had a family. It is difficult to imagine that the simple act of creation, the business of making a baby, could be grasped in a head so filled with theories, equations and scientific complexities.

'I was once the keeper of the Tsar's birds, of the royal aviary,' he begins, 'for I have always had a way with birds, a natural affinity, even if I say so myself.'

I nod, remembering the incident with the breakfast crumbs, though I can see that this information surprises the others.

'As the royal ornithologist I was visited by bird salesmen from all over the world carrying cages of exotic birds. The great blue and yellow macaw, the exotic keel-billed toucan, and the crimson topaz hummingbird from South America. The noisy pink and white galah and parrots and rosellas of every colour from the Antipodes. From German New Guinea, the bird of paradise. Proud chickens with plumes as bright as peacocks and leg feathers of crimson and blue from China, and regal peacocks themselves from the forests where tigers roam on the slopes of the Himalayas in the Kingdom of Nepal. Grey parrots from the Congo River in Africa which live for a hundred years, and blue doves from the spice island of Zanzibar. From the bitter soda lakes of German East Africa, the glorious lesser pink flamingo.

'Men of every colour and creed came to my door – Africans, black as polished ebony wood with filed teeth and silver bangles banding their upper arms. Yellow-skinned Mongolians and shy, saffron-robed Tibetans, their eyes dark clove slits in flat calm faces. Turbaned men from Afghanistan with fierce hooked noses and eyes as hard as tektite. Men from Bolivia draped in brilliantly coloured blankets who wore bowler hats and smoked thin cigars which they held in slender coffee-coloured fingers.

'Tsar Nicholas took some pleasure in his aviary and I believe he thought it well worth the upkeep, which was considerable,

73

but it was his daughter Princess Tatiana who loved to come each morning to see the birds. She was a pretty little creature with a brilliant musical ear and she would spend an hour or more each morning talking to the birds. She could emulate to the exact tone, rhythm and intonation every bird call in the great glass-domed imperial aviary. And repeat the honks and quacks of the geese, swans and wild ducks which swam in the ponds and lakes created around it. She could as easily mimic the honk of the snow goose as she could the raucous squawking of a sulphur-crested cockatoo, and in the very next breath she might create the soft cooing of a blue dove or the call of the English nightingale. There seemed to be no bird call, no matter how strange, that didn't come to her ear naturally. The birds would flutter and dance excitedly in the air around her as she entered the aviary.

'To this remarkable talent Tatiana added another – an affinity with numbers. In this she was an equal genius.'

The professor pauses, looking up at the stars and allowing himself a sigh. 'If ever I had a child I would have wished it to be Tatiana, daughter of Tsar Nicholas. Indeed, I came to think of her in much these terms and could hardly wait for her to appear each morning when, after talking to the birds, she would take breakfast in the lodge with me. Here I gave her lessons in algebra and geometry and soon we had moved into the realm of higher mathematics and abstract equations. What a delightful mind the child had, and if Russia should ever have another queen, it will be well served if they should choose the Princess Tatiana.'

'Ah, that is not likely, there is an heir at last, the continuity of the Romanoffs is now assured,' Olga Zorbatov says smugly.

I think to myself, We are all fleeing from the tyranny of Tsarist Russia and here is Mrs Z being a royalist, pompous as anything. Besides, she is interrupting too much and now that the professor's story has changed from the names of silly birds it is becoming really quite interesting.

'Is it true Prince Alexei has a rare blood disease and will not make old bones, perhaps not even grow to be an adult?' I ask. I had heard this rumour from a monk at a monastery we had passed on our travels, who had sold us a sack of potatoes. He told me that one of their kind, a monk named Rasputin, had been selected by the Tsarina to be with the heir to the throne of all the Russians as his spiritual healer, and that God had granted this monk the gift of stopping the boy from bleeding to death. I did not find this altogether strange, for it has been my observation that the Gentile God is very involved with blood in one way or another.

'That is correct, the prince is a sickly child and often covered in bruises and there is a lot of loose talk. More than this I cannot tell you,' the professor says and then adds, 'though I admit to having been told a little more in the utmost confidence.'

'Then it is true!' Olga Z says triumphantly, shaking her head up and down and pouting her lips. 'A queen for Russia, eh?'

'That is not what I said, Mrs Zorbatov, it was only a chance remark. Tatiana is a remarkable young lady, or was, until the Indian myna bird came into my life and completely spoiled our relationship.' The professor scratches his head and says ruefully, 'Now that I am gone from her life, one must suppose she will be taught needlework and how, with good grace, to bear intolerably boring conversations.'

This last remark stops the speculation about the condition of the Prince Alexei, heir to the Russian throne, and we all grow silent. The professor is about to get to the juicy bits.

The Indian myna bird is a most unprepossessing bird, not much bigger than twice the size of a sparrow with dull brown and pale yellow breast feathers, though it has a bright eye ringed with black and a lively, busy manner. It gives the impression of intelligence as it cocks its head at human sounds and seems naturally curious. It is easily tamed and can be made to learn tricks and to emulate a number of expressions of the voice, so that there are those who believe not only that it can learn to speak but that it can understand what is being said as well. I must point out to you all that this is not true; the Indian myna, like the parrot, can learn sounds if they are constantly repeated, but has no comprehension of their meaning.

As I said before, it was the habit of the Princess Tatiana to take breakfast at my lodge, which also served as the gatehouse to the greater bird sanctuary. It was here that the bird salesmen with their exotic species would come. Princess Tatiana would often accompany me to the gate to look at the day's offerings. Sometimes she would urge me to purchase a rare and beautiful specimen, and after I had carefully examined the bird to see that its feathers hadn't been dyed or new ones skilfully sewn to old with minute stiches or gummed to truncated quills I might do so. But first I carefully questioned the salesman as to the bird's habitat so that we might place it in a climatic condition within the great glass aviary where it was most likely to survive.

On the morning of the Indian myna bird we had been offered several fine specimens, including, as I recall, a rufous-tailed jacamar from the tropical rainforests of the Amazon which I was obliged reluctantly to refuse. It is a bird that lives mostly on butterflies and the butterfly house in the aviary had for some reason, probably a malfunction of the temperature, destroyed all that season's butterfly pupae. The chances of our keeping the jacamar alive through the winter were not very good, while the price being asked for the exotic bird was not inconsiderable. Despite the disappointment of the Princess, I was forced to conclude that the Tsar's money could be better spent elsewhere.

We had all but concluded our inspection of the birds for sale that day when the princess stopped at an enormous gilded cage beside which sat a most imperious looking man on a small carved stool. At first appearance he seemed to be an Afghan, though in some respects different. He had none of the savage, bearded looks of the fierce mountain people, nor was the ubiquitous rifle slung about his striped, ankle-length jalabi robe. Whilst his nose carried the distinctive hook of an Afghan tribesman he wore a neat moustache and a well-clipped goatee. He had bowed his head respectfully when the Princess Tatiana approached, though he did not kneel and place his forehead on the ground, nor did he rise to bow with his hands clasped.

I was first alerted to the situation when I heard the princess laugh and I looked up to see the large and, I must say, rather ostentatious cage. 'Look, Professor, a little brown bird of no value whatsoever and even less charm in this big and silly cage,' she called out to me.

She had barely said this when I heard her laugh again, but as I could see her lips I knew at once that this second laughter, so like her own, came from the small brown and yellow bird with black ringed eyes and bright yellow legs which appeared a trifle too long, as though they should belong on a bigger bird.

The princess looked in surprise at the little bird, then she clapped her hands. 'Oh we must have it!' she exclaimed. 'You must buy this laughing bird at once, Professor.'

'It is not for sale,' the man seated beside the cage said quietly.

'Come now, my good man,' I said, in a superior tone, 'I am not so easily duped; the bird has no value but the cage is of silver, though I'll vouch there is too much lead in the mix.

It is the cage you wish to sell, is it not?' I did not wait for his reply before continuing. 'Well, it is the bird we want and you may keep the gilded cage and sell it to some silly, degenerate nobleman of which Russia has far too many splendid examples.'

Tatiana giggled. The royal palace was constantly filled with slack-mouthed suitors from the nobility, some of whom would have great difficulty counting to the sum of their bejewelled fingers.

The Oriental ignored my rudeness. 'The bird is a gift from the Queen of Persia for the Princess Tatiana but it must be won by her in fair competition,' he said quietly.

'Competition? A gift to be won? Who will challenge Her Royal Highness?' I laughed at the indignity of the proposal. 'The Queen of Persia? And what in and what for?' I sniffed. 'The prize, a silly little brown bird?'

'The Indian myna bird is not a silly little brown bird and this one is bred of generations of Persian royal birds. It has an astonishing intelligence. The challenge will be at mathematics and bird calls!'

I must say I did not care much for his arrogant and confident manner, but before I could protest the princess exclaimed, 'I should like that, I should like that very much indeed!' She turned to me. 'Professor, you must invite our new friend to breakfast in your lodge where the competition will take place. I shall order something nice for him from the kitchen, and you and I will have English porridge with honey as usual.'

'No, Princess,' the turbaned gentleman said quickly. 'The Queen of Persia has sent sweetmeats from the Orient. I will try this thing you call porridge and you must eat of our food which I know will delight your palate.' He rose slowly and extended his hands to show a ruby ring on each forefinger with a Cyrillic script carved into the stone. 'I am the brother of the Sultan of Arabia, who also sends you greetings.'

It was plain to see that Tatiana was impressed. After all, it is not every day you meet a Sultan of Arabia's brother.

'We shall have to call the royal taster and your governess and at least two referees; I shall be one and another must be found,' I said.

'By all means,' the sultan's brother said. 'Will you allow my servant to accompany me?'

We had barely noticed the presence of the bearded little man who stood quietly some paces behind the sultan's brother.

'Certainly,' the princess said. 'He can also be the second referee if you like.'

The sultan's brother smiled. 'He is only a servant, Princess, he will carry the cage and then sit at my feet and sleep.'

The servant carried the great gilded cage into the lodge and set it up in the breakfast room behind a chair where the sultan's brother was invited to sit. Then, clasping his hands together as though in prayer, he bowed to us and took his place cross-legged at his master's feet where he appeared almost instantly to fall asleep.

The royal taster and the governess were summoned, together with one of the royal accountants who had come to work early. Soon the table was covered with the most exotic food. Chocolates and Turkish delight and all manner of dried fruits and nuts and little sweet cakes, all of this supplied from a great bag the sultan's brother's servant had given to my servant. Wine was brought for the adults, though the sultan's brother asked for water with a little juice of the lemon added.

A plate of steaming porridge was brought for him along with a goblet of water. He dipped a spoon into the porridge, lifted it to his imperious nose and sniffed. 'No smell? Perhaps just a hint of honey?' Then he tasted it, though very tentatively on the tip of his pink tongue. He pulled a face, more a polite grimace, and then placed his spoon down. 'I have already eaten,' he said, handing the plate back to a servant to take away. He waved his hand across the table filled with eastern delights. 'Eat, please. Enjoy, compliments of the Queen of Persia.'

I'm not at all sure I was happy about the way he was taking over and I must admit it was a very strange breakfast. But the princess seemed happy enough and seemed to relish all sorts of delicious bits and pieces, and soon declared herself wonderfully satisfied even though the royal taster looked decidedly sick from the rich food.

'Now for the competition, Sultan's Brother,' Tatiana said. 'How do the rules go?'

'No rules, just sounds and numbers. You may keep the Indian myna bird if you can make a bird sound with your throat or make up a mathematical calculation it cannot repeat exactly or answer accurately.'

I laughed out loud. 'Sir, your bird is soon lost!'

'Shall we make a wager on that?' the sultan's brother offered gently.

We all laughed. 'You do not know what you are saying, sir, the princess is gifted in emulating the song of birds and also in mathematics. Besides, we are servants of the Tsar and cannot wager money on his daughter.'

'Oh, but I can!' Princess Tatiana cried. She turned to the young clerk. 'I have money of my own, money sent to me by Queen Victoria and other money, have I not?'

The accountant nodded his head glumly, not at all sure that he was authorised to make expenditure on behalf of the young princess.

'Good! Then, Professor, you shall wager for me!'

The sultan's brother reached for a leather bag somewhere in his striped robes and counted ten English gold sovereigns onto the table. 'Shall we start with only a small wager? I do not wish to embarrass the princess.'

I looked at the ten gold coins in dismay. 'I do not have the authority!' I stammered.

'Yes you have, I just gave it to you,' Tatiana cried. 'Let's get on with it, please, Professor.'

'I only have the Tsar's money, which I use for the purchase of birds,' I said helplessly.

The princess sighed and clucked her tongue. 'You will be repaid every kopek should I lose, which I shall not.' She turned to the sultan's brother. 'Shall we begin? What bird call shall I make, Professor?'

I placed ten gold coins on the table to the value of the English sovereigns. 'The Common Potoo, *Nyctibius grisues*,' I replied. This strange relative of the nightjar can be heard on any moonlit night and comes from tropical South America. It has a most difficult-to-emulate warble of several notes, as though three or four different birds are in harmony, and it is one of the bird calls Tatiana found at first most difficult.

Almost at once the strange, plaintive cry of this ugly little bird which, as a matter of interest, has the additional ability to distort its body so that it might appear to be a part of a log or a wayside stone, came from the princess. It was well delivered and those around the breakfast table who heard it smiled, as it was indeed a most complex call.

Our smiles were almost instantly wiped from our faces, for Tatiana had barely drawn breath again when a precise emulation of the sound came from the myna bird. My ear for birdsong is perfect and both the princess and I knew that we had lost our wager.

The sultan's brother added my coins to the pile in front of him. 'Shall we wager double your last two bets on the next call?'

'Yes, yes, the English nightingale, a complete stanza!' the princess exclaimed, clapping her hands gleefully.

Almost immediately she started to warble the beautiful notes of the nightingale's call. It was an enchanting sound and masterful in its rendition, and brought tears to the eyes of those who listened. But no sooner was it over than the little myna bird repeated it perfectly. The sultan's brother raised his eyebrows at me and I was forced to nod, then he took the twenty gold coins from my side of the table and added them to the pile in front of him.

'No more!' I cried. 'We have seen enough. You may take your myna bird away with you, we do not need a bird who can sing like all the other birds, we have a Russian princess who can do that!'

Tatiana looked dismayed. 'But we have hardly begun, Professor!'

'Princess, we have lost thirty gold coins, not quite a king's ransom, but the better part of my monthly budget for buying birds.'

'But I told you, Papa will pay! I have my own money, we haven't challenged the bird to any maths!'

'Shall we say sixty gold coins, double what you have already bet?' the Oriental man, whom I was beginning greatly to dislike, suggested. My heart beat faster as I observed the pile of gold coins on the table in front of him. To add sixty more would be to take my entire budget for the summer.

'No, no, I really must insist.' I looked for help from the accountant but he avoided my eyes and reached over for a piece of Turkish delight.

'Oh just one more, please, Professor, just one truly hard one.'

The sultan's brother's hand rose. 'The rules for mathematics are different. I will give you a problem and then you will compete with the bird to see who can most quickly solve it.' He pointed to me. 'So that there is no suggestion of prior knowledge – that is to say, the bird has already been taught the answer – you, Professor, shall set the second problem.'

I shrugged and counted out sixty gold coins from the velvet bag on my lap, and when I had laid them before me I knew that only two more coins lay in the bottom of the bag. I had spent four years' salary for a mathematics professor at the Moscow academy where I had once taught.

'Sixteen multiplied by 29.5, divided by 11.5; subtract 6 and multiply by 77,' the sultan's brother announced.

It was child's play. If this was the sort of maths the myna bird could do we would win all our money back and all that of the odious Oriental. Tatiana would make short work of such a problem, in thirty seconds or less. The seconds ticked by and the bird hopped in what appeared to be some agitation from one perch to another. 'Two thousand, six hundred and ninety-eight, point three four – do you wish the continuing decimal places?' the princess shouted triumphantly.

'The princess is very clever,' the sultan's brother said quietly and pushed all the coins back over to my side of the table. I was profoundly relieved. Princess Tatiana was capable of much better and it was my turn to create a complex equation. 'Shall it be double again?' I asked, looking at the one hundred and twenty gold coins in front of me.

'Of course,' the Oriental said, though I thought with a little less enthusiasm.

I set a new problem much more difficult than the one set by the sultan's brother, one which was, in fact, at the extreme limit of Tatiana's capacity. It would take her two minutes or more of mental calculation and I sat back to wait, thinking of the fortune we were about to earn. But in less than twenty seconds the bird had the answer.

The sultan's brother rose from his chair and swept the golden coins into a leather satchel. 'There is a matter of two hundred and forty gold coins to come from you, Professor,' he said.

'I cannot pay you now, you will have to take a promissory note.'

I turned to the accountant who shrugged and wrote out the note, insisting that I authorise it with my signature.

'Thank you,' the sultan's brother said. He rose from the table and kicked the servant who lay asleep at his feet. The little man seemed to wake up with a start and scrambled to his feet and from his pocket took a handful of corn which he scattered on the floor of the cage. Then he stood to rigid attention beside the gilded cage as the Indian myna bird pecked busily at the granules of corn. The sultan's brother bowed to us all, last of all to Princess Tatiana.

'You have been most hospitable and I thank you. As a token of my esteem, and that of the Queen of Persia, you may ask the royal myna bird any question you like about your own future, for, in addition to its other talents, the bird possesses the gift of prophecy.'

'Please, we have had enough, I must ask you to leave at once,' I said sternly.

The sultan's brother looked down his imperious nose at me. 'Be calm, Professor, there is no wager involved in this.'

'Any question?' the princess asked excitedly. She seemed not in the least concerned at losing so much money.

The sultan's brother nodded.

'About the future?'

Again the sultan's brother agreed.

'Will I grow up and meet a handsome prince and live happily ever after?' Princess Tatiana asked.

We all looked to the bird which had suddenly and in great agitation flown up to its perch and commenced to chirp in the familiar and unpleasant manner of the common Indian myna bird. Not a single vowel or consonant which might be mistaken for human language escaped from its beak as an answer to the princess's question. Then it did a last frantic flutter and dropped dead, falling off its perch to the bottom of the cage, its over-long yellow legs pointing skywards.

'A terrible omen!' Mrs Zorbatov exclaims. 'It dropped dead, the bird died, can't you see? It *is* the prophecy, the Princess Tatiana is going to die!'

We all look at each other in horror. While we have no time for the Tsar, me least of all with my whole village destroyed and my people killed by his Cossacks, we nevertheless wish no harm on the beautiful Princess Tatiana, who seems to us the first intelligent Russian royal since Peter the Great.

'That was some bird!' I say at last. 'Some schmarty-pants bird!'

The professor shakes his head. 'It wasn't the myna bird who was smart, it was the professor who was stupid! You see, it was the Oriental gentleman's servant, he was the smart one, a brilliant mimic and a ventriloquist, not to mention a mathematical genius.'

'Oh yes? Well, what about the bird dropping dead like that, then?' Olga Zorbatov challenges. Like all of us she wants the Indian myna bird to stay smart so the story won't lose its mystery.

The professor sighs. 'The corn was poisoned, the corn the servant threw into the bottom of the cage killed the bird.'

The remainder of the story I shall tell, for it was the reason the professor was included in our group of refugees fleeing from the Tsar's secret police.

Like most young women the princess had become over-excited at the prospect of the competition, and when the professor visited the royal exchequer to claim the money she had promised, his request was promptly denied and he was confronted with the promissory note he had signed. When the young accountant and all the other witnesses were called in, they, for fear of becoming implicated, denied that the princess had agreed the money be used for gambling purposes and that she would repay it from her own pocket. As for the princess herself, she simply wasn't asked if she had authorised the professor to act as he did. Despite his pleas for her to appear on his behalf, this too was denied to him.

The professor was arrested and thrown into jail for the fraudulent use of the Tsar's money. He was sentenced to twenty years in Siberia but escaped from the train when a guard shook him awake in the early hours of the morning. The engine had stopped to take on water. 'Go!' the guard whispered urgently, pushing the professor off the train. 'The Princess Tatiana can do no more than this for you. There is a troika waiting which will take you to a remote hamlet fifty kilometres away. Arrangements have been made for you to winter there, if you do not freeze on the way. When the thaw comes you will be on your own, and remember, if you are caught you will be shot!'

89

Little did we know as we sat around the fire that night that not many years later the Tsar and the Tsarina and Prince Alexei, the haemophiliac heir to the throne, the Princess Tatiana and her four sisters would all be shot, murdered by the Reds in the Russian Revolution of 1917.

Maybe the corn was poisoned, maybe not. Maybe by dropping dead, that clever Indian myna bird was trying to tell the Princess Tatiana something after all?

**1 × 1.5 kg/3 lb chicken
pieces**, all skin and visible
fat removed

**2 tablespoons fresh
ginger**, finely chopped

2 cloves garlic, finely
chopped

peel of 2 mandarins,
pith removed

10–12 dried apricots

¼ **cup/65 ml/2 fl oz soy
sauce**

**1 cup/250 ml/8 fl oz
chicken stock**

¼ **cup/65 ml/2 fl oz dry
sherry**

black pepper, freshly
ground

1 tablespoon cornflour,
mixed with cold water

Savoury
Aviary

RECIPE

METHOD

Preheat the oven to 190°C/375°F/gas mark 5.

Lightly oil a casserole dish and add all the ingredients except the cornflour. Toss to coat the chicken pieces with the sauce.

Bake for 35 minutes in the preheated oven, turning occasionally. Just before serving, add the cornflour mixture to the sauce and stir over a gentle heat until it thickens.

Serve with rice or noodles.

Serves 6

The
Banquet of
Past Suffering and
Future Joy

Olga Zorbatov is a seamstress, or so she says,

though she has not been observed with so much as a needle and thread in her possession since coming to us.

Her only interest seems to be in matters gastronomical and verbal, for she is constantly preoccupied with food and chatter. She is also most contrary; no matter what one says, Mrs Z feels compelled to take the opposite viewpoint.

For example, if we are fortunate enough to have sufficient beetroot to make a nice borscht soup and someone observes that it is a little lacking in salt, Mrs Z will immediately declare it to be too salty for her taste.

She has grown quite thin, which is only a manner of speaking for she is still a big woman but much trimmed down and even more healthy than when she first joined our group.

How very fat she was at that time, with double and even treble chins. A person shouldn't call another person fat; that is, if such a thing can be avoided. But with Olga Zorbatov, believe me, fat was a compliment. She would wobble like a great jelly as she walked and we all feared she would slow us down, for she had the greatest trouble keeping up and often lagged behind the professor who uses a walking stick and suffers from arthritis in his hip.

But she is not without courage and, besides, she has a strange gift. She is a remarkable scavenger and, most days, seems able to prophesy where a little food may be found. Quite how she does this is a mystery and we are often forced to shake our heads in amazement.

We will be travelling on the road and in the distance and to our left might be the dark line of a pine forest. Mrs Z will stop suddenly as though she is sniffing the air.

'Mushrooms!' she will announce. Then she will turn to the children. 'Take a big basket, look carefully under the trunks of the larger trees, brush away the dead pine needles, you'll find them there.'

If our resident mushroom expert, Anya, is feeding her baby and won't accompany them the children go reluctantly, kicking at stones and looking back over their shoulders. These are children gathered on the way, orphans and strays from the bigger towns who are unfamiliar with nature and do not like entering dark woods and, besides, there is always something scary about a pine forest. But sure enough, they will return in an hour or two with much excitement and present me with a basket brim-ful of wild mushrooms.

The strange thing is that Mrs Z seems to know in the morning before we go scavenging whether there will be extra food to find during the day's long journey. She will point in a direction when we are all ready to set out, and we know now to obey even if the path seems at first to be quite wrong. Soon enough we'll come to a wayside apple orchard with wind-blown fruit scattered under the trees.

Or she might point to a swamp and say, 'Goose eggs!' and the children will scamper off and return several minutes later with a clutch of large eggs. Occasionally she'll point to a green water-hole in a river almost dried up in the summer heat. 'Fish over there and biting!' she will announce. Sure enough, Mr Petrov, the blacksmith, who is our resident fisherman, will soon land a fat carp or two for our dinner.

It is quite uncanny, especially as Mrs Z knows nothing of country matters and can't tell a farm goose from a Muscovy duck unless it has already been plucked and dressed by the butcher. I once asked her how she came to have this second sight for the whereabouts of food, which I must point out she lacks in everything else and is much more likely to rush in like a bull in a china shop than to be in the least sensitive to the feelings of the others.

'I see it in the stars,' she said. Seeing my bemused expression she continued. 'Since the death of my husband, God rest his soul, I sleep little at night.' This was true enough, I would often wake in the night to find her walking about, muttering away and gesticulating to the sky. 'I watch the sky and speak to my husband, Sergei, who tells me in what direction we must travel in the morning to find a morsel to eat.' Mrs Z looked at me, one eyebrow slightly raised. 'Last night Sergei was riding on the tail of Pisces and today Mr Petrov caught three fat fish!'

It is best to mind your own business when you are travelling with others, even though I admit I am not very good at it. I nodded my head as though this revelation were a perfectly satisfactory explanation. If Mrs Z was a little soft in the head, what did it matter? Who was I to question her astral conversations with her dead husband? Why should I care if he had his head stuck in the jaws of Leo the lion, or rode on the tail of Pisces the Fish, when the results were of such benefit to all of us? So I kept my mouth shut and said nothing to the others because now I knew definitely Olga Z was crazy.

So when she put up her hand to tell a story, given her passion for food and her verbal dexterity, her astral connections and her lively imagination, crazy or not, I anticipated a star performance. Little did I know how right I would be, though none could have suspected the strange tale she was about to tell us.

This is Olga Zorbatov's story as told to us under the stars somewhere in Russia in the summer of 1909.

'There are many ways to use an astrological chart,' she begins, 'and almost all have to do with personality. We are all born under an astrological sign and there are some people who believe that we are trapped within our signs. For example, the child born under Leo on the zodiac chart is said to be a natural leader. Someone born under the Scorpio sign is thought to have a sharp tongue and a peremptory manner. Taurus the Bull makes for one impetuous and unthinking, likely to tramp over people's feelings. If you are born under the sign of Aries the Ram ...' Mrs Z pauses and looks a trifle embarrassed, 'you are said to be … er, good in the bedchamber.'

This brings laughter from all of us. Then Mr Petrov, the blacksmith, who is responsible for the fine fish stew we are going to enjoy tonight, asks Mrs Z if she was born under the sign of Taurus.

'How did you guess?' she says, plainly surprised. Mrs Z seems confused when her remark causes a further gale of laughter.

Olga Zorbatov continues. 'Now this would be very well if it worked, but how often do we find a Leo person as timid as a mouse and quite unable to make a decision? A Scorpio who is completely unselfish and lives to be in the service of others? Or a Taurus like myself who is not in the least clumsy and by nature sensitive? Do you get the idea?'

We all nod, trying hard not to laugh.

Well, this apparent contradiction worried my husband, Sergei, who was a cook and also an astrologer with a growing reputation. 'Olga, sweetheart?' he said to me one night as we dined on the roof of our small house at midnight under the stars. You see, he would come home late from his work as head chef in the kitchen of the Hotel Grande Rex in Moscow which, as you must all know, is where only the highest of the Russian nobility are to be seen dining. Upon returning home from the steaming atmosphere of the great kitchen he liked to partake of a meal at midnight in the open air under the stars. Though, of course, this was only possible in the summer.

'Yes, my beloved, what is it?' I replied.

'Look!' Sergei said. 'How brightly Taurus the Bull shines tonight.'

I spread goose pâté on a small slice of fresh soda bread and poured vodka into the silver horn he loved to use as his goblet and handed both to him. 'It burns bright for you, my beautiful husband.'

'Taurus is never overly bright in the Moscow sky,' the professor says suddenly.

'So now already the Birdman of St Petersburg is telling this story?' Olga Z asks, appealing to all of us.

'On that particular night it burned bright, Professor!' I interject.

'So, let me continue.' Mrs Z turns to the professor. 'With

your permission, of course, Professor-of-little-brown-birds-that-make-a-fool-of- so-called-clever-men!'

'We must have no more interruptions, please!' I say sternly.

'Thank you, Mrs Moses,' Olga Zorbatov says. 'It is nice to know there is somebody civilised here! If you remember, before I was so rudely interrupted, my husband was about to speak.'

'Olga, sweetheart, I have a theory that Heaven is the great kitchen of human possibilities, and that the stars are the cooking ingredients and the signs of the zodiac are the dishes of the personality. We astrologers have it all wrong, people are not trapped within their astrological signs. It is more likely that if we are born under a sign, we can use the characteristics of that sign to effect good or evil on others. A Leo, for instance, can teach his children the principles of leadership, which is good, or he can be so adamant about being the leader that he can bully his family and rob them of initiative forever, which is bad. For instance, you, who are gentle as a lamb, are born under the sign of Taurus the Bull, but you do not choose to be impetuous and unthinking, which is bad, but steadfast, loyal and protective, which is good.'

I picked out a *gozinnakh* from a small silver platter and popped it into his mouth. This small ball-shaped confection, as you all know, of course, is made entirely of chopped nuts, honey and sugar. 'You are so very clever, Sergei. When did you come upon this brilliant theory that the heavens are the great kitchen of human possibilities?'

'By watching people eat. There is a saying among chefs that people are the food they eat. Watch what people eat and you will at once know a great deal about them.'

'And what does this have to do with the stars?'

'Simple. If you change what they eat, you change what they are! If a woman has been completely dominated by her husband who is a Leo, the meat eater, she will be forced to eat too much meat and her diet must be immediately adjusted, because every time she eats meat she will feel much burdened by her husband's personality.'

Even an ignorant country woman like myself can see that there are several holes in this astrological argument and I can hear the professor snorting in indignation to himself. But we dare not interrupt for fear of upsetting Mrs Z further, and this theory of her husband's also makes some sort of crazy sense.

Sergei was born under the sign of Sagittarius the Archer and was therefore obsessive and single-minded and always aimed straight at the target of his particular ambition. Taking our modest savings he opened a small sanatorium which was centred around a magnificent kitchen. He let it be known among the noble customers of the Hotel Grande Rex that, through the practice of astrological dietary discipline, he could change difficult personalities for the better and also cure depression, aggression, fits, ravings, suicidal tendencies, lost memory, uncontrolled weeping, coarse language in women, and all the various moods and mental frustrations and aberrations commonly found in persons of noble lineage.

The nobility were only too pleased to find somewhere to dump their misfits and in no time Dr Zorbatov, the self-titled Professor of Astrological Science and Zodiac Law, found he had more patients than he could handle. Princes, grand dukes, generals and counts paid huge sums just to gain a few places nearer the top of the waiting list.

The curious thing was that it appeared to work. Not in every case, as some patients had lost too many marbles too long ago for anything to be done, but in a great many less grievous situations.

Sergei worked out an astrological dietary regime for each patient, but only after having cast an astrological chart of the patient upon admission, and this chart, taken together with a great deal of close questioning about the patient's family and family history, determined what they should eat. He had a vast knowledge of food and herbs and the effect various cuisines have on the human body and mind and he used this to great effect.

Often the patients would enter the sanatorium in poor health and in a few weeks or months they would be different people, their symptoms eliminated. Those who had entered fat and flaccid would leave with a trim waist and in the best of health.

My clever Sergei also came up with what he called his 'patient dialogue', and as the sanatorium grew larger he employed people from the academy who were studying the new science of the mind to listen to the patients and make notes as they spoke of their pasts. Often they would uncover a history of early beatings or cruelty, or sexual abuse from a father or an uncle or even an older cousin. And it was from these sessions that he invented his master therapy, the Banquet of Past Suffering and Future Joy.

This was a grand affair, a banquet to which the patients were required to invite themselves when they felt ready. If they volunteered, believing themselves sufficiently recovered to undergo the routine, they were counselled as to the nature of the dishes available. There were twelve dishes in all, divided into six 'good' dishes and six 'bad', each of the twelve corresponding to a sign in the zodiac.

Each dish symbolised a personality characteristic which could be associated with a particular astrological sign. Though, as I have said, Sergei believed that there are good and bad aspects of every star sign, for the purposes of his banquet, the bad dishes represented the worst aspect of its sign and the good dishes the best.

There was the Aries pie, a dish made of mutton and in particular the meat of a ram. This pie represented the sexual drive gone wrong and sexual abuse of a small child.

Then there was a huge beef steak which was named the Tyrannical Taurus, which represented the bully and the tyrant.

Then came a chicken soup which, strangely enough, represented Scorpio, the sign of the Scorpion, for while it tasted delicious it was extremely hot, laced with fiery red peppers so that the tongue swelled in the mouth. This dish stood for temper and subsequent beatings, love promised and then withdrawn, duplicity and betrayal.

The Coil of Cancer was a length of sausage a metre long which lay coiled like a snake upon a white plate and was filled with every imaginable flavour given to sausages. It represented mysterious stomach pains, headaches, temporary blindness, uncontrollable temper tantrums, depression and other mental maladies which lacked a ready explanation.

Under the sign of Leo was a dish of raw meat thinly sliced and seasoned with herbs, pepper and capers and served with hot English mustard. It stood for undue severity and unreasonable control and the demand for unquestioning and absolute obedience.

Finally on the list of 'bad' dishes came the Capricorn stew, a dish which took after the goat it represented. In fact it was made of goat's meat, but as the goat is known to eat anything it contained just about everything which could safely be contained in a concoction cooked in the juices of meat and vegetables. Capricorn stew represented any past and negative afflictions visited upon the patient which he or she had not yet discovered or spoken about.

These six dishes were collectively known as the Food of Sorrow.

Then there were the astrological dishes which contained positive characteristics, those traits to which most humans aspire. These were known as the Food of Joy.

The Gemini twins were represented by a dessert known as Gemini Gloriana, a dish wonderfully sweet to the taste but the odd spoonful of which would be distinctly tart. It represented a natural easygoing personality, not easily upset but, if given a just cause, not incapable of responding.

Virgo the Virgin was a lemon sorbet, delightfully fresh tasting and clean to the palate. The characteristics it represented were openness and innocence.

Aquarius, the Water-carrier, was simply a large crystal jug of pure spring water with a tincture of various Oriental herbs added. It represented vigour, decency, sobriety and good health. Aquarius was also symbolised by a bowl of fresh fruit, and the additional characteristic this added was a sweetness of disposition.

Pisces was a salmon pâté, extremely subtle to the taste, and it represented the salmon who swims for so long against the stream and stood for individuality, determination and character.

Sagittarius was not a dish but a clear white wine with a most beguiling bouquet and a clean, delicious flavour. A single mouthful went straight to the blood to produce an invigorating effect which turned easily into laughter. The characteristic it represented was constant good humour.

Finally there was Libra, the Scales, a most popular dish though it was not a dish at all but a pair of scales which allowed the guests to take equal amounts of any two dishes so that they weighed precisely the same. This allowed for a mix of positive characteristics. For instance, a hundred grams of lemon sorbet taken with a fresh pear promised a sweet disposition and a charming and innocent nature, a combination much liked by the female guests at the banquet.

All this talk of food, even the kind that represents the bad characteristics, is making us exceedingly hungry and the fish stew Mr Petrov has made is tugging at our nostrils. It is time Olga Zorbatov concludes her story or we will soon be completely famished, though how her tale will end is a complete mystery and she has, in my mind anyway, already received very high marks for storytelling.

Well, now that you know the dishes served at the Banquet of Past Suffering and Future Joy, it remains only for me to explain the procedure.

On the afternoon before the banquet the patients were taken into a small garden known as the Garden of Past Suffering, which led off from the banquet hall. Here they were given silver trowels with their name etched on the blade and made to dig holes to the depth of their arms and then a little more, so that by reaching into it they were unable to touch the bottom. Though the soil was soft enough and easy to dig, most of the patients had never handled a trowel in their lives and took to the task with little expertise. But, despite their grumbling, they were not allowed to hand the job over to a servant as it was compulsory to complete the task themselves. The soil from the hole was then neatly piled beside it and the patient's name placed on a small paper flag which was stuck on top of the pile.

The banquet took place under glittering crystal chandeliers with all the trappings usual to a grand and important occasion. Musicians played from the Moscow Symphony Orchestra. There were jugglers and acrobats and exotic dancers and, at one stage, a full military band marched through the hall playing a march which celebrated the defeat of the British and French in the Crimea.

The patients, or guests, were dressed in all their finery, in uniforms and evening dress, the men wearing full decorations, and the women emblazoned with jewels. The crystal chandeliers made the tiaras on their heads blaze with light. At nine o'clock precisely the music ceased and the guests sat down to eat. The first astrological dish of their personal choice, the dish of negativity, was placed before each of them.

Dr Sergei Zorbatov, Professor of Astrological Science and Zodiac Law, addressed the glittering throng. By now he was an immensely rich and powerful man with friends in high places, the confidante of grand dukes, counts, generals and politicians. In a few short years he had brought more sanity into the Russian nobility than had existed for the past four hundred years. There was even talk that the Tsar would make him Minister for Culture.

'You will eat every morsel set before you; not one crumb, not one spoonful must be left of the dish you choose. This is an order!'

There was a loud groan from the assembled guests; the food set in front of them was more even than a starving peasant could hope to eat in a week in paradise. But such was the authority and esteem in which they held Sergei Zorbatov that they simply bowed their heads and started to eat.

They ate until they could eat no more, whereupon one of the observers, judging the time to be right, would place a bib over the head of a satiated banqueter and lead him quickly to the Garden of Past Suffering where he was made to stand beside the hole he had previously dug and marked with his name.

As each patient appeared in the garden, looking much the worse for wear, the professor would address him by his name and title. For example, he might say, 'Prince Nicolae Dimitri Pyotr Donskoy, you are here to be granted complete and unconditional absolution from your past. As a demonstration of this, the harm done to you, and the guilt you feel, will be expelled from your body and your soul and buried forever.'

A servant would then hand the prince a small crystal goblet of clear liquid which was a potion made from the castor oil plant. The prince, at Sergei's command to drink, would throw back his head and down the contents of the glass. Almost instantly he would buckle over and a moment later he would expel everything into the hole in front of him, vomiting every morsel of the negative astrological dish until he gasped and shuddered and spat repeatedly to get the last of the evil out of his mouth. Then he would be made to kneel and scoop up the soil and fill in the hole, in this way burying the past with his own hands.

When this task was completed a servant would bring him a bowl of warm water and a towel and he was allowed to wash his face and hands. Whereupon he was given a goblet of Sagittarius wine, the wine of invigoration and pleasant humour, and led back into the banquet hall where he would be placed at a second table with fresh linen, crystal and silver and presented with the astrological dishes of future sanity and peace of mind.

Olga Zorbatov looks up and shrugs her shoulders. 'That is my story,' she says simply, then, turning to me, 'Mrs Moses, the astrological fish we are eating tonight in the form of a stew smells delicious and I, for one, am starved!'

As usual it remains for me to complete the story and it was several weeks before I could pluck up the courage to approach Mrs Z. I would wake up during the night to find her wandering about talking to her husband who, it seemed, continued to gambol around the zodiac, for she had lost none of her second sight since the night of the story and we still depended on her to find that little extra to keep us from starvation. One night I awoke, it was a full moon and almost light enough to read a book. At first I heard and then moments later saw Mrs Z talking to the sky. I had seen this often enough before but quite why I decided this time to approach her I cannot say. I rose from my blanket beside the fire and, walking over, tapped her on the shoulder and said, 'Excuse me, Mrs Z, is there anything I can do for you?'

She turned slowly, as though she were in a trance. 'You want to know what happened to my husband, don't you, Mrs Moses?'

I nodded, too confounded to find the words.

'He was murdered.'

My hand went to my throat. 'Oh how sad! Was it one of the people who attended his sanatorium?'

'No, Mrs Moses, he was killed by a lonely and bitter woman who every night for a thousand nights and more waited on the roof, under the stars, for her husband. Each night she prepared a midnight feast for him consisting of the most delectable dishes and chilled a bottle of the finest vodka to drink from the silver horn he had once so loved.

'But her husband was too busy dining with dukes and sleeping with countesses and he had no more time to meet the woman under the stars. So the woman ate the entire midnight feast by herself and grew very fat and cried herself to sleep every night.

'And then one night he came to the roof. His hands clasped behind his back, he watched the stars and then he spoke.

' "Look, Olga, there is Taurus the Bull." He pointed to the night sky. "It is your sign."

'For a moment the woman's heart leapt and she took the silver horn and filled it with vodka and started to walk towards him, to forgive him. Her husband had come back to her and it would be like old times. Then he spoke again.

' "I don't suppose you can help being fat and ugly and clumsy, as bulls are naturally all of these unpleasant things." He turned around to face her. "My dear, I do not love you any more and have come to take my leave of you."

113

'It was then that she charged him and knocked him down and stabbed him through the heart with the silver horn. What else could she do? She was born under the sign of Taurus and she behaved in the only way a bull knows how when it is baited beyond endurance.'

1 kg/2 lb lean beef brisket

6 large carrots,
peeled and sliced

1 turnip, peeled and sliced

1 sweet potato, cubed

1 small onion, cubed

1 tablespoon golden syrup

4 medium potatoes,
parboiled and halved

1 tablespoon plain flour

salt and black pepper,
freshly ground

Balkan BEEF BRISKET

METHOD

Cut the brisket into 8 cm/3 in slices and place in a large casserole dish. Add the carrots, turnip, sweet potato and onion.

Pour in enough boiling water to cover the meat and vegetables, and simmer for 2½ hours over a medium heat on top of the stove. If the liquid has reduced too much, top up with more boiling water. Add the golden syrup and the potatoes, and simmer for a further 30 minutes.

Mix the plain flour with a little cold water to form a paste and add to the casserole, stirring until the sauce thickens. Allow to simmer for 3 minutes, then season with salt and freshly ground black pepper.

Serve with rice or dumplings.

Serves 6 to 8

The
Blacksmith
With a
Beluga Tongue

Mr Petrov likes to call himself a practical

man. When folk ask him what he does he shrugs his shoulders. 'I am a blacksmith.' He says this without pride and then adds deprecatingly, 'I put shoes on horses and fix handles onto cooking pots.' He once picked up the Family Frying Pan and held it in his large fist, as though judging its weight and quality, and for once the old frying pan did not look too big for its boots! He grinned. 'A fine pan, Mrs Moses, the very best, solid as a blacksmith's head.'

I'm not sure what we would do without Mr Petrov; in such a bunch of misfits a practical man is badly needed. He can mend shoes, catch fish, cut firewood, trap small animals and birds, build a rope bridge across a rushing stream and make a snug shelter from bark and twigs. Without him, babes in the wood that most of us are, we'd be at sixes and sevens, completely lost. While this one argues with that one about how a project should be undertaken, Mr Petrov goes quietly ahead and before you know it we are saved from disaster once again.

Like Mr Mendelsohn, Mr Petrov is not a big talker and, again, both men have beautiful hands, the one for the violin and the other for mending things. Different hands to be sure. The musician's hands are slim and elegant, soft as a girl's from the city with long white fingers and nails neatly trimmed. The blacksmith's hands are broad and blunt, powerful hands with the nails broken and the palms calloused so that when he shakes your hand your fist disappears completely and you hope he doesn't squeeze it too hard. But that never happens, because Mr Petrov's hands have a gentle touch.

When Mr Petrov says quietly one night that it is time he told a story we are all delighted. Though I, for one, taking him for a shy but practical man, do not expect he'll be much of a storyteller. Practical people get on with things and, in my experience, they are seldom romantic and so, while we are pleased he is coming out of his shell, we are not exactly holding our breath for an earth-shattering début.

'I was born in a small fishing village,' Mr Petrov begins, 'on the banks of the Volga River. Its name is not important, there are twenty villages along our stretch of the shoreline and each is no more distinguished than the last. The fishing rights to a stretch of the great river were decided in ancient times and must be strictly observed, so that the life of a river fisherman is hard. Sometimes the fish disappear for weeks and the greatest prize, the noble sturgeon, may not choose to use your stretch of the shoreline for years. My family were poor and, like most Volga fishermen, always in debt to the caviar buyers from St Petersburg, Moscow and Persia and so they were determined that I, their only son, Petrov Petrovitch, would enjoy a less precarious vocation.'

'You are an only child? I too am an only child!' Pretty Tamara Polyansky exclaims in a surprised voice, as though being an only child is some sort of miracle.

'Shush, Tamara!' Olga Zorbatov says, as usual without a hint of good manners. Though for once we are all rather pleased; none of us want Mr Petrov to dry up from a sudden fit of nerves. Anyway, Tamara Polyansky is a 'Miss Showbiz' and once she gets started nothing can stop her gabbing on about acrobats and high-wire acts and dashing young men in very tight tights. *Oi Vey!* I should be so lucky! But this is no time for daydreaming or showbiz talk!

'I have five sisters,' Mr Petrov says quietly, 'and so being a boy and the youngest I was spoiled by them all.' He laughs. 'Nothing but being a blacksmith was good enough for me. A blacksmith's living does not depend on the widow-making sea or the unreliable coming of the sturgeon when, if time and tide and other vagaries coincide, they may chance to swim into the shallows near your village to spawn.

'Once every ten years this may happen on your particular shore and there is a killing for the village, but the occasional taking of the caviar, the roe of the sturgeon fish, is only sufficient to keep poor men still poor after they have paid their debts to the caviar buyers, bought new nets and perhaps a boat or a donkey engine, repaired the roof of their cottage and put aside a little for a daughter's dowry.

'It is the middlemen, the caviar merchants and dealers from Moscow and St Petersburg and the dark-eyed men who in the season come from Persia, who grow rich. All wear gold and diamond rings, shiny boots that reach to their fat knees and fine woollen coats that carelessly sweep the ground. Their hands are soft and their tongues oily and they can steal the nose off an honest fisherman's face without him knowing about it until he tries to sniff.

'And so I was apprenticed to a blacksmith. It was work I was well suited to do, for, while I was big and clumsy in the small fishing boats, I quickly adapted to the hammer and tongs. I took to the furnace and anvil with alacrity and did not miss the water too much. The blacksmith shop was near the river bank and I could look out and see the boats returning in the late afternoon, and see the ebb and flow of the mother of all rivers and witness the rhythm and the changing of the seasons and so never lose touch with the generations of family who had served and worked the Volga.'

Mr Petrov looks up at each of us in turn as though wanting to explain this last remark. 'You see, we have been fisher-folk since time out of mind, maybe for a thousand years, maybe more. Each year we pray the sturgeon will come to our part of the river, and we count ourselves fortunate if it should come once in three years. In the meantime we fish for less exotic fare and hope we catch sufficient in our nets to feed our families.' He smiles, a secret, even sentimental smile. 'If you cut me you will see it is salt water and not blood which runs through my veins.'

Professor Slotinowitz now interrupts. 'Did you know,' he says in that know-all voice he uses, 'that the sturgeon fish is one of the oldest animals on our planet and has existed in much the same form for a hundred million years? The cockroach also, which has existed for an equally long period with almost no further evolution; it is perfectly adapted for its function and environment.'

'Since when are a fish and an insect *animals*, Professor? A fish is a fish and an insect is a lousy bug!' Mrs Z proclaims.

'Enough!' I say, never mind my lack of tact, which, believe me, is a commodity now certainly not called for. 'Who is telling this story anyway? Mrs Z? Or the professor? Or Mr Petrov here?' I turn to Mr P. 'Please, continue, so far it is most interesting. I, for one, have never tasted caviar.'

Mr Petrov smiles at me. 'Ah, Mrs Moses, then you have not eaten from the table of God himself! A big fish, a mighty sturgeon, grows up to four metres in length not counting the snout, which, by the way, it uses as a tool to turn the sea bed for food. The big fish are known as beluga and give the biggest grains of roe, each grain as black as a South Sea pearl. A single tiny grain, no bigger than the head of a match, when placed on the tongue and pressed lightly against the palate will *explode* in the mouth and the delicate and exotic taste will remain for an hour!'

'My husband, the great chef, and I would eat it in great dollops on blini pancakes,' Mrs Z brags.

Mr Petrov pauses for a long moment. I glance over and observe to my surprise that the big, strong man, with hands that could throttle a bear, is crying. A bright tear runs slowly down both of his cheeks. He is by no means a handsome man, too many flying sparks and iron pellets have burnt into the flesh of his face, which is now a permanent ruddy colour and rough as coarse sandpaper, but his tears give him the vulnerable look of a small boy who is very sad. He slowly shakes his head. 'Excuse me, Mrs Z,' he says in a slow, measured tone, 'to *dollop* such a brilliant creation is to shit in the mouth of God!'

For once Olga Zorbatov is stunned into silence.

Mr Petrov becomes aware of the presence of his spontaneous tears and quickly knuckles the wetness from his eyes. 'You see, the tasting of caviar means a great deal to me,' he explains. 'It is the reason I am here, the first of my village's people to flee from Mother Russia in a thousand years.' He looks up at the night sky and sniffs again and then he looks back at us. 'You must all be thinking: What does a blacksmith know of caviar? You would be right – herring pie maybe, but not beluga caviar. No village fortunate enough to catch a big sturgeon fish would waste a single grain of its caviar on a humble fisherman, let alone allow a blacksmith near its precious beluga.'

Mr Petrov stops to think for a moment and for once there is complete silence from all of us, only the sudden crackle of a twig on the fire is heard. 'The very best of beluga caviar carries with it the word *malassol,* which is a fancy term but means only that it is lightly salted.' Mr Petrov then explains. 'A woman may add a pinch of salt to a dish she is preparing, stir and taste. If it is not salted enough she will add more until she is satisfied. If too salty she will add a little water. But with the best caviar it is different. The beluga can only be salted once and if the salting is not correct the whole batch is spoiled. You see, the process by which the best Volga caviar is salted is an instinct and a great gift. He who has this gift from God is named the Salt. He is a prince among the river fishermen and his gift is so rare that the old women light a candle in every village church on every day of the year and with it a prayer is offered to Saint Peter, the patron saint of fishermen, that the Salt lives to be a hundred years and that God's most precious gift, a beluga tongue, will be with him until the day he dies and goes straight to paradise, no stopping at the gate, no questions asked.

'When I was twenty-five, the Salt, on whom all the villages depended, died. He was very old, more than one hundred and seventeen years, and known the length and breadth of the great Volga River. It was claimed that he was discovered to have the beluga tongue at the age of eighteen, and for ninety-nine years it had never failed him and not a single batch of beluga caviar was ever spoiled in the twenty villages where he worked.' Mr P smiled to himself. 'Village children like myself grew up thinking of him as only next to God and the Tsar in ranking and, because we had not met the other two gentlemen personally, perhaps more important.

'At the news of his death all the village priests made a pilgrimage to the bishop's cathedral in the capital city, while we all rushed into the village churches to pray that God would grant us the miracle of another beluga tongue. The bishop explained to the priests the method they should use to find another Salt.

'The caviar buyers from Moscow, St Petersburg and from Persia were summoned to the convocation and informed that they must supply one hundred kilograms of the finest unsalted beluga caviar. This was in itself a king's ransom and the dealers argued and pleaded with the holy bishop to make it one hundred lots of one hundred grams instead. But the bishop held his ground and showed the greedy middlemen where the correct amount was stipulated in the ancient *Book of River Rights*, which was at least five hundred years old and was the final authority on how the Salt must be chosen. Finally, after much wringing of hands and crying poor, they agreed.

'The ancient method of finding a beluga tongue was quite simple. A hundred unmarried men must be picked at random and each given a kilogram of the finest beluga caviar. From this fortune in fish eggs he must pick a single tiny egg and place it, as the Salt has always done, on his tongue, and then he has to roll it around his palate and when it explodes he must decide the exact amount of salt needed in the dish set in front of him. If he gets it wrong he will have spoiled a fortune in the best beluga caviar and, no matter how great his skill, he will never again be included in a fishing boat that hunts the sturgeon. Of course, if he gets it right and is discovered to have a beluga tongue, his fortune is made and he will be a rich and honoured man until the day he dies.'

'Excuse me, Mr Petrov.' It is Anya Mendelsohn (she is not married to her violinist, but they are betrothed and she wishes to take his name) who speaks quietly, then waits for further permission. We are all very much surprised, she has never interrupted a story before. She holds her baby to her breast as Mr Petrov nods in her direction. 'Excuse me, please,' she repeats, 'but what does a man know of salting a fish dish? Surely this is women's work!' She waves a dismissive hand. 'A fish egg is a fish egg, roe is roe, salt is salt, taste is taste; so tell me, please, what's so special about this beluga fish egg that a good female cook cannot judge its salt?'

Anya's question makes sense and all the women look towards Mr Petrov, who has now suddenly turned a furious crimson colour. 'It, it, c-c-cannot be done by a woman,' he stammers.

'And why not?' Mrs Z demands imperiously.

'I, I, c-c-cannot explain,' Mr Petrov stammers again and it is obvious that he is mortified by Anya's question.

'But why not?' Anya asks in a reasonable voice. 'A woman is trained from childhood in these things, her palate is well used to tasting for salt and herbs and the absence or presence of the right quantity of all sorts of subtle flavours and secret ingredients.'

'Yes, like mushrooms!' Mrs Z says, ever the tactful one.

Mr Petrov is now even more visibly disturbed and bites his lower lip so that I think at any moment it will start to bleed. The perspiration is running down his brow and his hands shake even worse than before. 'Her blood, her m-m-m-monthly blood,' he stammers at last. 'Her b-b-blood will spoil the caviar for the whole season!'

There is a collective gasp and it is now our turn for embarrassment. We have forced poor Mr Petrov into an impossible confession.

'As a Jew I can understand this,' I say hurriedly. 'In our law a woman is unclean when it comes to that time of the month. She must take a bath in the *mikvah* and is forbidden to prepare food. Your Volga River fishermen would make good Jews.'

I look around and can see that everyone is grateful for this explanation and Mrs Moses, who is of course me, is granted top marks for tact and diplomacy. Then I say, 'Please, continue, Mr Petrov, tell us how you look for this person who will have a beluga tongue, which we now understand can't be a female, for what you already explained are very good and sound reasons.' I smile and in a cheerful voice say, 'If this caviar is as nice as you say, there must be a great many volunteers among the young men, I think.'

Mr Petrov is by no means a stupid man and he gives me a grateful look. 'No, no, no volunteers, Mrs Moses! The selection of one hundred men must be hand picked by God. The priest in every village, all twenty, must choose five unmarried men by a very particular method. In each village the holy father will select a tree or a rock or a point on the river bank or any object his prayers have pointed out to him in a vision, and he will go to that object and sprinkle it with holy water and anoint it with precious oils. This must be done in the dead of night when the village is asleep. Then the first five unmarried men in every village to pass this holy point which has been decided upon by God through his servant are the chosen ones.'

'But what if all should fail?' Mr Mendelsohn the violinist asks.

'Ah, that is the miracle! It has never been known to fail, there is always a new beluga tongue who comes to light. Saint Peter the fisherman has never deserted us.' Mr Petrov stops and absently scratches the tip of his nose with his forefinger. 'Except once, when the holy saint of all the world's fishermen picked the village blacksmith to be the new beluga tongue.'

'You!' we all chorus. 'You were the one chosen!'

Mr Petrov nods sadly. 'In our village the priest chose to sprinkle the holy water on the anvil. The blacksmith's shop is on the edge of the village and the fishermen, who rise at dawn to go to their boats, are forced to pass it. So, by accident, because I too rise early to fire the furnace, I was included in the first five men to pass the anvil and so was picked with four young fishermen friends to represent our village.

'On a prescribed day we travelled to the bishop's cathedral in the capital fifty kilometres away. When we arrived we were each given a small wooden disc with a loop of leather strung through it and told to hang it around our neck. On each disc was a number that also appeared painted carefully on the side of a white porcelain bowl which, first washed in holy water, was handed to us wrapped in new muslin cloth. We entered the cathedral and were made to sit cross-legged in rows on the marble floor and were then shown how to spread the muslin cloth in front of us and place the numbered bowl exactly at its centre. Beside it a priest placed a small bowl of white Siberian salt and a pair of tiny birchwood tweezers wrapped in new cheesecloth so that it could not be contaminated by being handled before it was needed. The bishop gave thanks to God and to Saint Peter the fisherman and said holy Mass and each of the candidates took the wine and the host from the hand of the bishop himself. Then all were required to drink from a silver chalice of water and to use this to rinse their mouth before spitting the water into a basin held by a novitiate. Then, when all this was completed, the cathedral doors were locked, and into each bowl was measured exactly one kilogram of precious beluga caviar.

'In front of us was the finest unsalted beluga, each bowl more valuable on the markets of the European cities than all the money any of us might earn in a lifetime. In just a few minutes all but one kilogram of the food God created to be eaten in Heaven would be destroyed by the addition of too much or too little salt. We waited for a final blessing from the bishop and then the salting of the beluga began.'

Mr Petrov stops and looks around at us. The food in the Family Frying Pan is almost cooked and even though we are all hungry I can see that there are none among us who do not wish him to continue.

I have mentioned the procedure before but I will repeat it in just the way it happened to me. With the wooden tweezer I selected a single fish egg, a single precious grain, a tiny pearl of glory, and placed it carefully on the tip of my tongue. I had never before tasted this priceless jewel of the sea and now I rolled it around my palate as though by some ancient instinct. The tiny ball of glory seemed to dance on my tongue and skate across my palate as though it knew exactly where to go to stimulate my taste buds. Then, quite suddenly, there was an explosion in my head as loud, I swear, as a single cannon shot fired beside my ear. With it came a burst of the most glorious flavour. My eyes rolled back in ecstasy and I began to moan with a strange pleasure. My arm lifted of its own accord and to my surprise I saw that I now held the tiny wooden spoon. Then my hand moved, again without any conscious effort on my part, and dipped the wooden spoon into the bowl of salt and sprinkled the salt over the beluga caviar in the bowl. Then, without hesitation and as if by magic, it returned and dipped once more into the salt and added yet another spoonful, then again, though this time slightly less than half a spoon. Still inwardly directed I mixed the salt into the beluga, my hand movements so slow my fingers seemed hardly to move at all. All this without a single thought entering my head and then, when the mixing was complete, my hand collapsed into my lap and lost all its power so that if I had wished to raise it to add more salt to the beluga I would not have been able to do so. All that lingered was the taste of the single sturgeon's egg in my mouth.

I have no idea how long I sat waiting for the cathedral bells to ring, for I seemed to be in some sort of trance. But then at last they rang out and the great doors were flung open and we rose and were ushered out into the great square to wait. It was now the dealers who would enter the cathedral.

There were twelve of these rich caviar merchants in their long woollen coats and shiny boots. They were known as the Twelve Apostles of Beluga, and they were responsible for the tasting of the salt. Five were chosen from Moscow, five from St Petersburg and two from Persia. Each had been selected for his immense knowledge of the sturgeon's roe and the exceptional clarity of his taste for the finest beluga caviar. Each carried with him tiny tweezers made of pure gold with which he must now select a single egg from each of the hundred bowls and, having tasted it, mark it for its perfection of salt. No word was spoken between them and they would simply write down the number of the bowl they had selected and hand it to the bishop.

You may imagine my surprise when a priest came hurrying from the cathedral calling out my number! The decision by the Twelve Apostles of Beluga had been unanimous and soon, with the cathedral full to overflowing and the bells ringing, the bishop announced my number again from the high altar.

Everyone claimed it was a miracle. A blacksmith, not a fisherman, had been given the beluga tongue by Peter the saint of all fishermen. In all of history such a thing had never happened before. Some of the old *babushka* immediately forecast that no good would come of it. But, of course, they were ignored, as most old women are in these modern times. 'The holy saint of fishermen,' the bishop explained, 'works in his own mysterious ways.' I was proclaimed the Salt of the twenty villages with a great ceremony and a procession that led through the city streets and which was followed by a banquet held by the caviar merchants and attended by the city's most important dignitaries. The food was much too rich for a blacksmith's palate, the vodka was of such a purity that it must have been distilled from the tears of God.

In my own village we feasted for days on herring pie, roast lamb and sweetmeats of every kind. I was a hero who had put our village on the map and brought great honour to all our fisher-folk. Henceforth, no beluga fish would leave our stretch of the Volga without first having been salted by me.

Needless to say, I was forced to give up blacksmithing, for I was a rich man who owned a horse and trap, and wore shiny boots and a coat that touched the ground. The candles in the village churches were lit for me with prayers for my good health, and children stepped aside and cheered as I passed. There seemed no end to my good fortune, except for one thing – the Salt must by holy tradition remain celibate and I would never know the joy of a woman in my bed.

I told myself that if a priest could take a vow of chastity and keep to it all of his life, then I too could overcome the primitive urge which conquers the minds of the strongest men. I was of a strong will and single-minded in my endeavour to live up to my vocation and commitment to my people. To strengthen this resolve I reminded myself that I had been granted the gift of a beluga tongue from Saint Peter the fisherman himself. I counted myself fortunate to have five spinster sisters to attend to my needs, and thus I possessed all the blessings of a married man save for connubial bliss.

As to the job at hand, it seemed I was truly gifted. On every occasion I was called upon to travel to a village where they had made a killing of the sturgeon it was the same. I made no conscious decisions, but no sooner had the precious jewel, the tiny black marble of sublime perfection exploded on my tongue when my hand, moved by the Holy Spirit, was guided to the salt pot by the Great Fisherman himself. The salting of the beluga was always performed to perfection and the term *malassol* on a blue can of Volga caviar from our region of the river became especially prized by the caviar merchants.

Within a few short years my name had become a legend right up into the furthermost reaches of the Volga. All the big, important fish, the most precious and glorious beluga, carefully packed in ice, were brought from far beyond our river boundaries for me to sanctify with the gift of salt.

And then one day, as I was travelling in my trap to a village not ten kilometres away where they had taken two great beluga fish that very morning, I saw a young woman limping at the side of the road. Her hair was the colour of flax and braided around her head in so many strands that, if it were allowed to fall, it must surely have reached well beyond her slender waist. She looked up at me as I passed and her eyes were the colour of the summer sky, though they were filled with pain and distress.

I quickly brought my trap to a halt, climbed down, and walked the short distance to where she stood. She bowed her head and modestly averted her eyes as I addressed her.

'Good morning, little sister, are you hurt?' I asked gently. 'Where are you going?'

Without replying to my first question she gave the name of the village to which I myself was travelling.

'Come, you may ride with me, my name is Petrov Petrovitch and, while I am a big fellow, there is room in my trap for both of us.'

'I cannot, sir,' she said, without looking up. 'I am not a married woman.'

'But you are hurt, people will understand.'

'My father will beat me, it would not be correct.' She looked up for the first time and smiled and it was as though an arrow had struck through my heart. I know this mention of Cupid's arrow is not an original idea, but there is no other way to describe the sensation. One moment my heart was beating in my chest as calmly as the ticking of the gold watch attached to the chain strung across my stomach and the next it was as though ... well, as though it had been struck through by an arrow!

I swallowed hard, attempting to stay calm. 'Do you know who I am?'

'Yes, sir, you are the Salt,' she said quietly, her eyes once again downcast.

'Well then, your father will know you are safe with me. Come along, I will help you up into my trap.' I took her arm by the elbow and she limped to the trap. I could now see that she was in considerable pain. I held her by her slim waist and lifted her into the seat. My big hands seemed to enclose her whole waist and I could feel the warm flesh under her coarse linen skirt and, I am ashamed to say, my throat tightened and went suddenly dry and I was forced to cough in an attempt to conceal my extreme agitation. Seated on the trap seat, her ankle was now at the level of my waist and I could see that it was red and inflamed.

'You have sprained it badly, perhaps even broken it,' I said clumsily, my voice sounding strange to me, as though it had risen another octave.

'No, sir, it was a scorpion.'

'A scorpion!' I exclaimed in dismay. It would take us half an hour of hard driving to get to her village. I looked again at the ankle and saw that the area around her foot and ankle was rapidly turning a deep scarlet as the poison was carried upwards to her heart. The sting from a large scorpion can kill, and now I saw the two tiny marks where the creature had struck her on the arch of her instep, injecting its deadly poison directly into the vein that lies near the surface of the skin. It is a large vein, I have since learned, called the Long Saphenous, and stretches from the instep up the entire length of the leg and is an easy ride for the blood pumping its way back to the heart.

I looked up at the girl and knew at once that we could not make the distance to the village in time to save her life. All fishermen carry a sharp gutting knife on their belt and, though I was now thought to be a gentleman and was never a fisher-man, it was a habit I had carried over from childhood when I had worked on the boats.

I reached for the knife and at the same time spoke to the girl. 'I am going to cut and try to suck the poison out.' I grabbed the buggy whip which had a handle of plaited leather and handed it to her. 'Here, bite down hard onto this!' She nodded, but by now the pain was so intense that she moaned and sobbed and her hands shook violently as she took the small leather whip and bit down hard onto the handle.

I cut deep into the scorpion sting, opening the flesh on the instep where the vein is still fairly small and even closer to the surface. Putting my mouth against the wound I sucked and spat. I continued for several minutes, tasting her blood in my mouth and spitting it onto the ground at my feet. I hoped I had acted swiftly enough to suck most of the poison from the vein.

At one stage I glanced up at the girl and saw that she held the handle of the whip clamped between her teeth and that her eyes were tightly closed against the pain while her cheeks were wet with tears of distress. My heart went out to this beautiful young woman who was suffering so much. I continued to suck and spit for another five minutes and then I took a small flask of vodka from the pocket of my coat and poured a little of it on the open wound and then held my thumb hard against the vein to stop the blood flow. I rinsed my mouth with a swig of vodka and spat the contents out and then removed the whip from the girl's mouth. 'Here, drink!' I said, holding the flask to her lips. Even in her state of distress her lips were soft and inviting and, I am ashamed to say, I felt the stirring deep inside me again and the pain in my heart returned. She parted her beautiful lips to take the vodka and coughed as the fiery liquid reached her throat, but she managed to keep it down.

I removed my coat and placed it over her shoulders and wrapped it around her to keep her warm, and then tore the sleeve from my shirt and made a tourniquet above her knee, blushing violently as I raised her skirt to tie and tighten the bandage. Tearing the remaining sleeve from my arm, I bandaged her foot. Then I leapt up into the trap and we set off at a furious pace for the village.

You can see I am not a small man, and the seat of the trap was not very wide, and so her body, wrapped in my coat, was forced against mine. Although the coat was of fine heavy wool and, I now tell myself, I couldn't possibly have felt her body through the thick material, it was as though she wore nothing and the firm flesh of her thigh were pressed against my own, and, despite her condition, I thought I must surely die of the pure ecstasy I felt at the proximity of her warm flesh. I could do nothing to stop the feelings that coursed through my blood and the terrible beating of my heart and I prayed silently to Saint Peter the fisherman to make my thoughts pure and stop the ache in my throat.

Twice on the way she vomited, but the tourniquet effectively cut the blood supply from her leg so that by the time we reached the village it was clear that I had been successful in sucking out most of the scorpion's poison and that she would live.

I carried her into her father's cottage and instructed her mother to remove the tourniquet above her knee. Her brother was sent to fetch an old crone who knew how to treat a scorpion bite, and I departed, but not before learning her name was Katya Markova.

'It is a love story! A beautiful love story!' Tamara Polyansky cries, clapping her hands together. 'Mr Petrov, you had fallen in love and ...' She stops mid-sentence; no doubt Miss Showbiz with the slow-motion brain has suddenly remembered that women are forbidden to someone who possesses a beluga tongue. Tamara now brings her hand to her mouth, which has formed into an 'o' of consternation. 'Oh dear, I am so sorry, I am so very sorry, Mr Petrov,' she says in a small, pathetic voice.

Mr Petrov sighs, then smiles a sad smile and spreads his hands. 'You are quite right, Miss Polyansky, I was hopelessly in love. Head over heels in love, besotted and enchanted and unable to think of anything else but the beautiful Katya Markova.'

In a week the news had spread around the villages and the village priest came to see me. 'Is it true, Petrov Petrovitch?' he asked.

'Holy Father, I am pure in my heart,' I told him. 'I have not taken Katya Markova into my bed, but I cannot deny she has entered my heart.'

'You cannot have her, Petrov Petrovitch, you are the Salt. Would you destroy the livelihood of twenty villages for a silly girl?'

'Father, I have prayed to God and to Saint Peter the fisherman all night for four nights that my heart will be mended, that the love I feel for Katya Markova will be taken from me, wrung

from my heart like a sea sponge, for I don't know how I shall
endure the pain of it if it should continue much longer. I am
aware that I cannot have her and I will live with this and pray
that God will forgive the thoughts in my head and the desire in
my heart. I shall swear on the Holy Bible that I will not take
Katya Markova to my bed and will remain the Salt for as long as
I am needed by the river people.'

'Bless you, my son! You will one day enter the gates of
paradise to the clapping of angels' wings and the sounding of
loud trumpets!' Then he added, 'A woman is a wonderful thing
for a man to possess, but a beluga tongue, now that is something else!'

Mr Petrov looks up and shrugs and it seems he has come to the
end of his story, which, I must say, I don't consider a very good
ending. The boyski doesn't get the girlski and all that's left is a
fish mouth? What kind of garbage is that? A miserable ending,
no less!

'So tell me, Mr P,' I say in a sweet voice which hides my disappointment. 'You remained the Salt and you told us before,
you were rich and famous and daily candles were lit and
prayers said on your behalf and you drove a horse and buggy
and wore shiny boots up to your knees and a pure wool coat
that swept the ground, so how come you're sitting on that log
with patches on your *toukis*?'

The others all laugh, but in a good-natured way. Mr Petrov

has three patches on the back of his trousers and each is of a different colour, one red, the other blue and the last brown. He is a practical man, but for neatness and sewing he knows from nothing.

'That is a very good question, Mrs Moses.' Mr Petrov looks at the Family Frying Pan bubbling on the fire and then at all of us, knowing that we are all hungry and that the food is ready. 'That is, if you are still interested?'

'Y–es … er,' everyone says, but in a tone which contains a certain degree of politeness, and I can see that the demands of an empty stomach are greater than the need for another empty ending.

'A good ending should not be served to an empty stomach,' I say. 'First we eat and then the ending will be even more satisfying.'

So, after we have eaten – turnips and cabbage mixed with a little fat and with three large potatoes, not so bad – Mr Petrov concludes his story.

'With the story of my love affair with Katya Markova put to rest by the priests in every village church, who, no doubt instructed by the bishop, all preached a sermon about the triumph of the spirit over the needs of the flesh, honour and dignity was restored. Candles burned again at the altar of Saint Peter the fisherman, giving thanks to the saint for having saved the situation. The general conclusion among the fishermen was that a beluga tongue is a great blessing and, besides, is a gift from God and the saint himself, whereas a woman is only gossip and trouble and, in the end, no gift at all.'

'Ha!' Olga Zorbatov snorts.

'But what of Katya? Does she love you? Is her heart broken?' Tamara Polyansky asks.

'It is a complete mystery to me that Katya should love a great clumsy person like me,' Mr Petrov says. 'But from the first moment she saw me after she recovered from the scorpion sting it became obvious to all that she only had eyes for me. That our love was a precious thing that had been made in Heaven.'

'You made the right decision, the economic welfare of twenty villages was more important,' the professor announces. 'No question about it.'

'More important than love?' Anya asks, incredulous. 'Nothing in the world is more important than love, Professor!' Then she adds in a soft and disappointed voice, 'You made the *wrong* decision, Petrov Petrovitch.'

'There is more,' Mr Petrov says.

Two weeks after the scorpion incident, news came from Moscow that the consignment of beluga I had salted directly after leaving Katya at her father's cottage had arrived spoiled. Three days later from St Petersburg another angry message: the caviar from twenty great beluga fish, the biggest catch of the season and worth millions of roubles, and all salted by me, had also arrived spoiled. And then more and more, every beluga

fish I had touched from the day of the scorpion was found on its
arrival to be unfit for consumption.

There was only one answer possible and it was contained
within the heads and spilled from the lips of every villager. I
had told a lie and had secretly taken Katya Markova into my
bed.

The rumour soon spread that I had been seen in a cornfield
with her and that I had lain with her, was making love to her
when the scorpion stung her on the instep. I had broken my
vow and lied to a holy priest and therefore to Saint Peter and to
God Himself! I had destroyed them all and must be destroyed
myself and all that I possessed should be given as a penance to
the church.

It was the rough justice of the fisher-folk and would be more
merciful than the torture and humiliation the caviar merchants
would demand. I would simply be taken out on the great river
and dropped over the side of the boat too far to swim back to
the shore.

I was forbidden to see my beloved Katya, but allowed a visit
from my five sisters. I forgot to tell you that my parents had
passed away several years before. There was a great deal of crying and distress for me but I knew, at least, that my sisters
would be well taken care of, even though they would forever
remain spinsters. I had publicly disgraced my family and there
could be no forgiveness, not even the poorest peasant would
take such soiled goods as his bride. Before the priest came to

confiscate all my possessions I had buried gold coins in a secret place which they had been told about.

As they took their leave, Anna, the oldest of my sisters, kissed me and whispered, 'God be with you, Petrov Petrovitch, and have mercy on your soul. We have decided to use the money you have given us to emigrate to New York and we will take Katya Markova with us so she will be safe.'

I was taken out at dawn, when the autumn mist hung over the great river. Twelve of the village elders, all fishermen except for the priest, accompanied me in the fishing boat. After two hours, when we had reached the centre of the widest stretch of the Volga, the donkey engine was cut. The men sang the great song of our river and the priest heard my confession. When I did not confess that I had made love to my beloved Katya Markova he demanded that I do so.

'You will not be granted absolution, my son. You will forever burn in hell! You must confess at once!'

'Holy Father, I cannot confess to what I have not done!' I cried.

'Lies!' one of the fishermen shouted. 'How else could the caviar spoil? Not once, but twenty times!' There was a chorus of approval at this remark. But I would not confess. Saint Peter the fisherman would know I was telling the truth and he is a greater authority before Almighty God than a village priest.

So they threw me overboard and started the donkey engine and in a moment the boat was lost in the mist. I knew that soon

I must drown, that the strength in my arms would eventually forsake me and that I would sink under the gloomy grey water a kilometre or more from the shore.

But God is good. I struck out for the shore, thinking that I should rather die exhausted than give in to my fate and simply sink to the bottom of the river. I had almost reached the end of my strength when I bumped into something floating in the mist. A large heavy object, which I grabbed, though it was not easy to hold onto it. It was a beluga fish, a dead sturgeon of great size floating on the surface. I was fortunate, for it was early autumn, the water was not yet freezing. Two days later we reached the estuary to the Caspian Sea, a distant shore well beyond the twenty villages and, like Jonah himself, I was saved by a great fish sent by God.

'It was her blood!' Tamara Polyansky cries suddenly. 'The blood you sucked from the scorpion sting! It was a woman's blood and it caused the spoiling of the caviar!'

Mr Petrov shakes his head and laughs. 'No, not so, my dear Tamara Polyansky; we Russians are a superstitious lot, and circus folk are, I believe, even more so, but there is a simple explanation. As I floated downstream holding onto the dead fish I saw many others also floating in the river. There was a mysterious disease among the sturgeon that year – this is now a well-confirmed fact – the roe of the precious beluga carried the disease and, though it could not yet be tasted in a single grain of caviar, it was already spoiled long before I salted it.'

We all applaud this splendid ending.

'And now we know your destination when we get out of Russia,' I declare happily.

'Yes, Mrs Moses, that is quite true,' Mr Petrov replies. 'I shall go to New York to find my beloved Katya Markova.'

3 salted herrings or 6 matjes herring fillets

1 medium white onion, grated

2 medium Granny Smith apples, grated

6 Marie biscuits, crushed

½ cup/125 ml/4 fl oz white vinegar

1 tablespoon sugar

3 eggs, hardboiled

3 dill cucumbers, finely sliced

S<small>ALT·</small>
·<small>OF·THE</small>·
S<small>EA</small>
Delight

METHOD

Soak the herrings in cold water overnight, changing the water occasionally. Wash and drain them, and pat dry. Remove the heads, tails and bones, and chop roughly. If you are using matjes fillets, wash them well in cold water and pat dry.

Combine the herrings, onion, apples and biscuits. Add the vinegar and sugar to taste, mixing well. Spread the mixture onto a flat plate.

Shell the eggs and separate the whites from the yolks. Finely chop the whites and push the yolks through a sieve. Sprinkle the chopped whites over the mixture, then the yolks.

Fan a few slices of dill cucumber on top of the egg strips. Serve with plain crackers or challah.

Serves 6 to 8

Miss Showbiz and the Death of Count Tolstoy

MISS SHOWBIZ, TAMARA POLYANSKY, COMES TO ME

this morning. 'I'm ready,' Mrs Moses, she says.

'About time, if I may say so.' I say this not without a little bite of sarcasm. 'The others have been gone nearly an hour trying to find tonight's meal.'

'No, not ready for that!' she exclaims with an impatient toss of her head, as though food, our greatest need, is only a trifle of no concern. She has her hand around the top of a sack and now she bends and grabs the bottom corners and upends it. Out roll potatoes and beets, half a sackful, and not one bad or mouldy. 'There! Satisfied?' she says smugly.

I am astonished at such a rich haul, but I can't let her see my surprise. 'Where did you get them?' I demand.

It's funny me talking to Tamara like this. I am the youngest of us all, not yet twenty, and Tamara is twenty-six and very pretty with green eyes and blonde hair – a real Russian, that one.

She's worked in the circus, her body is as supple as a snake's, and that one knows her way around men, even with someone as flirt-proof as the professor. The children say she can do a double backflip, then a somersault and land back on her feet, just like that. But personally I have not seen this. If I did, I would wonder what a lady was doing throwing her legs around and being definitely indecent in terms of what she shows in the process.

'I'm sorry, Mrs Moses,' she now says. 'I was doing my stretching exercises and forgot the time.'

I point accusingly to the vegetables at my feet. 'You haven't been out this morning, so where did these come from?' I ask again.

Tamara Polyansky shrugs her pretty shoulders. 'I don't know, the sack was there at my feet when I woke this morning.'

Unlike most of us, Tamara still cares about her looks, and her hair is neatly braided, her face scrubbed and her lips stained carefully with blackberry juice. Even her patched dress and coat somehow look more stylish on her thin body than Mrs Solomon's still excellent coat looks on me. She is not a Mrs but a Miss and, unlike myself, doesn't pretend otherwise.

I sigh and give her a hard look. 'Tamara, God is good, and with His help we will maybe someday get out of Russia, but so far He hasn't started to leave food in a sack at our feet when we wake up. Who gave you this food?'

It is hard being a leader. It would be so nice sometimes just to follow for a while. You know, just put one foot in front of the other knowing somebody else is doing the thinking and taking the responsibility for our safety, patching up the quarrels between people and worrying about what we will find to eat every long, tiring day on the road. Sometimes, when I feel the stretch and the itch of the large purple scar where the Family Frying Pan burned through my flesh when we were running away from the Tsar's marauding troopers, I wish that the so-called miracle of the invincible Mrs Moses had never occurred. But then, on the other hand, I think, I'd be dead from the first soldier's sword thrust into my back. So never mind a little scar; compared to being dead, I must say here and now that being the leader of this bunch of no-hopers is definitely a lot better.

Now I look steadily at Tamara Polyansky and my eyes narrow. 'It was the boy from the village, wasn't it? That young man who followed us all yesterday afternoon? Followed you! You could practically see his tongue hanging out and not only his tongue!'

Tamara lowers her eyes and nods her head. 'I swear I only gave him a little kiss, a tiny peck on the cheek.'

'A kiss? Then another kiss and then another and what follows after these kisses is a kind of acrobatics you also learned in the circus, eh?' I say accusingly. 'You have put us all in terrible danger, Tamara Polyansky!'

Tamara's eyes brim with tears. 'He … he, looked just like my Eugene, the spitting image.' She begins to sob. 'I couldn't help myself, it was just a little kiss. Like kissing a beautiful ghost!'

'We are in danger!' I shout. 'Terrible danger! We have to leave now! At once! Go and find the others, tell them there is already food for tonight. Never mind the mushrooms, we have to leave immediately!'

'But why?' she protests.

'The village boy stole the beets and potatoes; if he is caught he will say we stole them. They will then come out and kill us!' I have seen how Russian peasants behave before and I am angry, but at the same time I can't help wondering what a kiss feels like. In my village the first kiss you get from a man is on your wedding night. Kissing is strictly off limits at all other times and occasions. Maybe that's why I am so angry with Tamara and her ghost kisser. Here she is kissing and smooching like it's going out of style, and I'm stuck with leading a bunch of misfits out of the wilderness. I call myself Mrs and I've never even been kissed.

'I'm sorry, Mrs Moses, I didn't mean any harm. I swear it was only a kiss, nothing more.'

Yes, young lady, for you only a kiss, I think to myself. For me it would be an earthquake. But on the outside I stay calm.

'Maybe it was just a kiss. As a matter of fact I believe you. But this young man goes back to his village and boasts of your kiss. You know how it is. He tells all his friends and he hints it was, well, *more* than a kiss, a *lot* more than a kiss, and he rolls his eyes and gets a dreamy look on his stupid face. They drink a little vodka and next thing they all arrive, all the young men from the village, with one thing on their minds, and it isn't a sack of potatoes and beets!' I give her this second explanation, knowing it is another possibility.

'I didn't think, Mrs Moses.' She stamps her foot. 'I am so stupid! It will not happen again. Please! If you make me leave I will surely die!'

'For God's sake, woman!' I yell at her, mostly so she can't see I'm jealous. But I am also worried; I have seen what a group of drunken peasants can do. 'Go fetch the others, we have to get moving!'

Tamara grabs me and gives me a quick hug. 'Thank you, Mrs Moses, thank you from the bottom of my heart.' She leaves, running in the direction of a small forest of birch trees where Olga Zorbatov has been directed by her husband in the sky to find blackberries and mushrooms.

We will have to retrace our steps, I think to myself. We will go back around the village we passed through yesterday in a wide circle, so that if we are followed by a gang of sex-crazed youths or angry villagers they will think we have moved on further down the road. It means two days lost, maybe three. This is our second summer on the road and I must try to get us out of Russia before another winter comes.

It is late afternoon when I suddenly remember what Tamara Polyansky said to me in the first place, before the debacle of the ghost kiss: 'I'm ready, Mrs Moses.'

I approach her as we make camp in a small copse of trees

where we can't be seen from the road. She has avoided me all day and even helped Anya with the baby. 'Ready for what?' I ask.

'Huh?' she says defensively, thinking perhaps that I am back on the attack.

I smile to reassure her. 'Tamara, please understand. What happened this morning is completely forgotten, only to be remembered if you do it again! But when you came up to me this morning you said you were ready. Ready for what?'

'Why, to tell my story, Mrs Moses.'

I laugh. 'Tonight then, Tamara.' I give her a hug. 'I'm sure it will be very good.' A leader has to encourage also sometimes.

Tamara is wearing her good blue dress which has no patches, and she's combed her hair then plaited it into two neat braids which shine like spun gold in the firelight. She is very beautiful, and I think to myself that there is no point being jealous when someone is so far ahead in the beauty business.

I have dark hair with a funny blob of a nose and my mouth is too big, though I think maybe that I have nice eyes, dark but nice. But Tamara is tall with a beautiful bosom. As a matter of fact, when Mr Petrov was talking about his lost Katya Markova, who, remember, is also a blonde with green eyes, I thought she must be a bit like Tamara. But when Tamara tries to flirt with Mr Petrov, who is a big man and still full of vigour, she is no more successful than with the professor, so maybe not. When you are a plain-looking brunette all pretty blondes look the same. Titch! There I go starting to be jealous again.

Tonight we have eaten first, because Tamara has requested this. Her story involves a cake, a large pink cake, and, as she rightly points out, cake comes *after* fish with potatoes and mushrooms.

I almost forgot to mention the fish. Mr Petrov caught a large eel in the fishtrap he'd made and left in the river last night, so that when the ghost kisser came to visit Tamara and left his sack, it became more than just a potato and beet night. It was an eel night too, and when Tamara set out to find the group who went hunting for mushrooms they had already filled a basketful, so also a mushroom night. Some night, eh? So tonight, thanks to all these goings on, we have just completed a feast to remember. Now, with our stomachs full for the first time in weeks, we can only hope that the story of the pink cake doesn't send us all to sleep before we can taste a single imaginary slice. Tamara begins.

I was an only child and my father doted on me. He was a fur trader and he dealt almost exclusively in mink, sable and ermine, which he exported to Germany, America, France and Britain. He always said the Germans bought ermine because they were vulgar, the Americans mink because their money was new and they didn't know any better, while the French and the English, both much admired by my dear papa, bought sable because it was neither vulgar nor ostentatious, and cost considerably more than the other furs.

As you may gather, we were wealthy and lived in a big house with many servants. I was taught to do all the things rich little girls must do if they are to marry into the right kind of family which, in my mother's eyes, meant the next step up the social scale into the minor nobility. I was given private music, singing and dancing lessons. I learned about French cuisine and practised English table manners, and by the time I was twelve I could accompany my parents almost anywhere without causing them embarrassment.

Oh, yes, I almost forgot the most important part. To amuse a young child with too much energy, who didn't much care for the stilted movements of the waltz and the polite restraints of the polka, my dancing master, Eugene Wilenski, taught me a little acrobatics. A few backflips and standing somersaults, how to balance and walk on my hands. I would have liked to learn ballet but my mother had strictly forbidden this for reasons of her own, which she never explained to me. Eugene Wilenski came from a poor family. His brothers, sisters and parents were all acrobats and he, too, had been trained to the trapeze and gymnastics, but he was now a scholarship student at the Academy de Dance and thought to be a most promising dancer. The exhilaration of twisting and flipping in the air as though I were flying was the most wonderful experience I could possibly imagine. Eugene would demonstrate a tumble or a backflip and the timing required for a standing somersault, and in no time at all my supple nine-year-old body could make a fair replication of the movement. With a little practice I soon perfected it.

'One day I will teach you to fly, little Tamara,' Eugene would laugh. 'Fly without fear from the trapeze and to walk the wire in the sky!'

Of course, when my mother discovered me tumbling about and twisting in the air she was horrified. The young dancing master was immediately dismissed and replaced by an old man with a shiny bald pate and a dark waxed moustache curled up at the ends who called himself Monsieur Alberto. I remember the last two centimetres of the moustache were white, and reminded me of a smug cat licking cream. I hated him from the first moment. He spoke French to me all the time, but with a simply atrocious Georgian accent, and seemed immensely pleased with himself. I was strictly forbidden to practise acrobatics, and a single backflip discovered by one of the servants and reported to my mother would result in my being sent to bed without supper.

My mother made sure that Eugene Wilenski was expelled from the academy. I saw him by chance a few weeks later and asked him what he would do. He told me he had no alternative but to join the circus or the army as, without a certificate from the academy, he had no qualifications. I was very sad for him. I told him that one day I would grow up and be rich and I asked him to wait for me. 'I will marry you and look after you and you will teach me to fly!' Eugene didn't laugh, instead he touched my cheek lightly with the back of his finger. 'Keep practising, *moy mecha,* one day we will meet on the high wire and then go to the trapeze and we will fly into each other's arms.'

On my tenth birthday I was given a party, the same sort of party all little rich girls get when they're growing up. I remember a beautiful cake, and the wish I made when I blew out the ten candles set into its lovely thick pink icing.

It was an orange poppyseed cake with layers of cream and green marzipan. I took a deep breath and, to the raucous cheering and clapping of the invited children and assembled adults, I blew all the candles out without taking another.

'Make a wish! Make a wish!' they all shouted.

I closed my eyes and suddenly my imagination filled with people, clowns and acrobats, jugglers, dwarves, dancing ponies, a tiger which snarled and jumped through a flaming hoop, and a magician in a black frock-coat and opera hat just like my dear papa wore when he went to the theatre. And in my mind I could hear a voice and it was the voice of Eugene Wilenski, my young dancing master, and I looked up and there he stood on a high swaying pole which almost touched the canvas roof of the circus tent. And then I saw the high wire strung from the pole to another on the far side of the tent and he was calling for me to join him.

'Come, little Tamara!' he called in my imagination. 'I *must* have you for my partner, you must walk the wire with me and do somersaults in the air!' He stretched out his arms. 'Will you fly into my arms? Shall I wait for you?'

And then there was nothing and I heard myself saying, 'When I grow up I shall join the circus and become a trapeze artist! That is my dearest wish.'

All the adults laughed, except my mother. When all the guests had gone, I was sent to my room without any supper, which was no hardship as I couldn't have eaten another thing anyway. But my mother had instructed my nanny, an old family retainer who had been my mother's nanny, to punish me. She had one rheumy eye and five coarse hairs sticking out of her chin and she always felt that I was too forward. She mixed a glass of soapy water and made me wash my mouth out, and then forced me to swallow the last mouthful of suds so that I heaved and brought up the orange poppyseed cake, among other things.

The old hag admonished me. 'That will teach you to disobey your mother. You and that silly jumping and twisting, you will forget all that and grow up to be a perfect young lady, it is *compulsory*. Then you will marry into the nobility and that is all there is to it!'

'You are not my mother!' I cried.

'I speak for her,' she spat back. 'You will do as your mama says! Only peasants are tumblers and clowns!' She rose and took the night lamp with her, knowing that I was terrified of the dark. I recall how I cried myself to sleep that night.

Children are not given credit for strong emotions and, in my experience, seldom are taken seriously. Yet I realised that night, though I had no name for what I felt, that I had been in love with Eugene Wilenski.

Tamara Polyansky looks at us. 'You have all led such hard, dangerous lives, you must think I was some spoiled little rich girl. And, of course, you would be right. When I was growing up I never had to think about anything of importance. I had food and clothes and a warm bed, holidays in France and England – always in the winter so my father could show his furs. All these privileges I enjoyed without thinking them in the least extraordinary.' She pauses and looks again at the strange group gathered around the fire. 'I can see from your expressions that you think my desire to become a circus entertainer, a trapeze artist, was a child's notion, a little rich girl's fantasy, soon to be forgotten.'

Anxious to reassure her, I quickly say, 'Your life as a child is as strange to us as Mr Petrov's childhood in a fishing village or mine in a *shetl* beyond the pale must seem to you. So far, my dear, we are enjoying your story and also learning new things about you.'

'Thank you, Mrs Moses.' Tamara looks at me gratefully and then gives a nervous little laugh. 'I have to say that tonight, hearing myself talk of those days in the Crimea and contrasting it with what has happened to me since, it seems almost as strange to me as it is for you.' She sighed. 'Such a long, long, time ago, and yet only thirteen years!'

'The only significant measurement of time is experience,' the professor says suddenly. 'History does not record routine and only measures birth, disaster and upheaval in the chronology of our lives.'

For once I understand his point. The time span of my own life is measured by four disasters. One was the year the crops failed and the government confiscated all the food they could find in the Jewish *shetls* to give to those Russians who were not Jews. I remember how the old people in our village deliberately starved themselves to death so that we young ones could eat what food we could scavenge. Then there were three Cossack raids. The last one you know about, and, of course, it was the worst of all. Only I remained with any time left on the disaster calendar of life.

Tamara acknowledges the professor and continues.

You will recall that I told you of two of my memories of my tenth birthday party, but there is a third: I remember the presence of Count Tolstoy.

Tolstoy was already an old man and in poor health and had come to live in the Crimea. He had just published his great masterpiece, *Hadji Murad*, and my father, a devoted follower, had sent the great Russian genius a sable coat as a gesture of his admiration.

Count Tolstoy must have received my father's gift of the sable coat, and it being a pleasant enough, though very cold, day he had put it on and driven over to our estate in a troika – I can only presume to receive more admiration and adulation from my father, as it was unthinkable that the great man would actually express his gratitude to a fur merchant, a lower member of a society it was well known he considered totally corrupt.

Anyhow, on this afternoon when Count Tolstoy came over to our estate, he totally ignored the usual protocol. Tapping his malacca cane on the marquetry floor as though he were blind, and without removing his coat and top hat, he walked straight past the footman and the protesting butler, through the picture gallery, to arrive unannounced in the ballroom.

In fact, he arrived at the very moment I blew out the candles and declared my wish to be a circus acrobat.

'Bravo! An excellent wish, my dear!' Tolstoy declared. 'If more well-born young ladies became acrobats and more acrobats became aristocrats then the Russian nobility would not be the ridiculous circus it has become. He chuckled happily at his own remark, then declared, 'I have thirteen children, all of them born into the nobility, and there is not a decent specimen, not even a good clown, amongst them!'

Tolstoy then turned to where my father stood and dismissively flicked his magnificent sable coat with the tips of his fingers. 'Sir!' he acknowledged, almost imperceptibly nodding his great white beard. He completely ignored the presence of my mother who stood thin-lipped beside my astonished and adoring papa.

Scowling, Tolstoy said, 'I don't much like children, but that was a fine wish, young lady. Remember, my dear, faith and love require a brave heart and some daring.' Then the old man turned and walked slowly out of the ballroom, through the long gallery, out of the house and was helped into his waiting troika by his manservant, who wrapped a well-worn marmoset fur blanket around his master's knees. He then removed Tolstoy's top hat and placed a Cossack fur hat upon his bald head and wrapped a woollen scarf about the old man's face.

I remember watching my father, who had hitherto remained speechless, running down the steps, his shoes crunching in the snow, and shouting, 'A new blanket for the troika? A little champagne, Master? Some hot beef soup to take on the journey?'

Count Tolstoy removed the scarf from his face. 'Good God, man! Is there no end to your impertinence! I am a *vegetarian!*' Then he wrapped the scarf back over his face, settled into his cocoon of fur and was off in a snuffling of horses and jingle of sleigh bells.

Whereupon my poor papa was so overcome at this visit to our home from the great writer that his eyes brimmed with tears and he started to shake all over and had to be led back indoors and up the grand staircase on my mother's arm, sniffing and sighing and sobbing all the way to his bedchamber.

My mama was less than impressed by the intrusion. She had been completely ignored and humiliated by a member of the aristocracy and she was very angry. She returned to the ball-room soon afterwards. 'You and your little friends will eat a piece of cake and then they must go home! There is a gift for each of them and you must thank them all for coming.' Then, calling my old nanny over, she whispered into her ear and looked in my direction and smiled at me. It was a smile I knew well, cold as ice. It was only then I realised that she was also angry with me, though I could not imagine what I had done to upset her. As I cried myself to sleep that night I thought her anger couldn't simply be because I had made a childish and inappropriate wish, but that it must somehow have something to do with the silly old man who had so rudely interrupted my party.

My love for Eugene Wilenski never wavered and nor did my desire to become a trapeze artist, though I kept my determination to myself. So that when I ran away to join a circus, the wish I had made on my tenth birthday had long since been forgotten by my family.

We were on a business trip to Siberia, where we travelled part of the way on the Trans-Siberian Railroad, which was not yet completed, and thereafter by river steamer up the Irtysh River to Omsk where my father had come to bid at a fur auction. Though by this time he was also heavily involved in the wool trade and he had secured a contract to supply overcoats to the Tsar's navy.

Siberia is not a good place to start if you should decide to run away from home. It is filled with vast spaces with not very much in them, and a young runaway girl with a fancy accent and good clothes is easily noticed. But there was a circus playing in Omsk. In it were a team of acrobats and trapeze artists who were simply splendid and I made my mind up there and then to become one of them. At thirteen I was getting almost too old to train as an acrobat. I knew I couldn't leave it a moment longer.

For almost as long as I could remember, my relationship with my mother had been a difficult one, but my father had always indulged me and I would miss him dearly. He had never been unkind to me. Most merchants have little time left over for their children, but my father liked to have his family with him when he travelled and so I had perhaps seen more of him than was customary. In the three years since my birthday wish I had saved all the money my father had given me on various trips abroad and I now felt I had sufficient to bribe or buy my way into a circus. All I needed to find was a circus master who would agree to take me on.

For a few coins spent at a flea market in Omsk the previous afternoon I had purchased an outfit of second-hand clothes, and a motley collection of spare bits and pieces to make a change of clothes. These I stored in the battered suitcase also purchased at the markets. I knew that if I were too well presented the circus master might attempt to return me to my parents for the larger gratuity than the money at my disposal which would no doubt be involved.

Dressing in these clothes would suggest to the casual observer that I was a cut above a peasant, perhaps the daughter of a minor government official.

Leaving our hotel was simple enough, though I almost lost my resolve when I thought of my dear papa and how terribly sad he would become at my departure. But with the thoughtlessness of the young I convinced myself that, because he was utterly devoted to my mother, he would soon recover.

I had observed the location of the servants' entrance and so in the early hours of the morning I quietly slipped out, dressed in my second-hand clothes with a white pinafore and cap I had removed from a hotel laundry basket.

Fate was on my side. I arrived at the circus site at six o'clock on the morning of the day the circus was departing by river steamer to the small city of Pavlodar in neighbouring Kazakhstan, about two hundred kilometres away.

It took me two hours before I could persuade any of the circus folk to take me to the circus owner. All protested that the circus had no vacancies. Eventually a roustabout took me to the owner's caravan in exchange for a few small coins. When I stood before him I seemed to quickly convince him to take me on. In fact, he agreed almost the moment he discovered how much money I possessed. I was to learn that life is cheap in a circus and money everything. With all of my money in his pocket, I became a member of the circus. And, as the professor has so eloquently put it, the first upheaval in my small life began.

Circus life is hard for anyone; for a young girl who had scarcely tied her own hair ribbons, it came as a tremendous shock. I had to fend for myself from the first day and I was treated as the dogsbody. I cleaned out the animal cages, filled the barrels with sawdust, spread it, swept up, and washed the dishes after the acrobats had eaten. In return, I was allowed a few crusts from their leftovers.

Circus people all work hard and are constantly hungry, and living off leftovers was a very precarious business. In a circus you only eat when you become useful and useful means being a part of an act. I was taught nothing but learned a lot just by watching. For the first year, while we travelled throughout Kazakhstan, I cried myself to sleep every night on a bed of straw under the tiger's cage.

'You slept under the tiger's cage!' Olga Zorbatov exclaims, clearly astonished. 'The *tiger's* cage?'

Tamara laughs. 'It was safe, smelly but safe.' She looks mischievously at us. 'Tiger's piss stinks twenty times worse than a cat's and besides, the tiger looked after me, she was my friend.'

'You became a tiger trainer?' Mr Mendelsohn asks, also clearly astonished.

'No, no, I had to clean out its cage and often I would help to feed it, and it got used to me being around.'

'But to sleep under a tiger's cage? In a circus this is normal?' I ask.

Tamara sighs. 'The only thing that is normal in a circus for a thirteen-year-old is that she is definitely not a virgin. I was pretty and my bumps in front were developing and I had a narrow waist and good legs and ...' She stops for a moment and then continues.

So, I slept under the tiger's cage. Tigers are nocturnal animals, they prowl all night up and down the cage. The tiger would snarl long before any of the men could crawl under the cage to get at me. I would always have warning and be able to run or scream, usually both, and the tiger would get very excited, and between me screaming and the tiger snarling and bumping against the bars of its cage the whole circus would be roused. The men who worked in the circus soon gave up and it was two years before I lost my virtue. In a circus, a fifteen-year-old virgin is practically an old spinster!

Believe me, if I could have run away I would have done so every day of that first year. But where could I go? We were in the middle of Siberia. I had no money, I had no means of contacting my father, though I suppose I could have stolen paper and pencil – not as easily as it sounds, I didn't even possess a kopek to pay for the postage.

I had sent *myself* to Siberia and I was a prisoner, just as much as if I had been locked up every night. I worked twelve, often as much as sixteen hours a day. But somehow I managed to practise the acrobatic exercises and well into my second year I began to understand the ways of the circus. I started to know what it means to be one of the circus people, how you are different, a separate tribe with a different language, a unique life; but there is a price to pay for every skill you learn in the circus, for every chance you are given. Nothing is given free, learning must be hard-earned or it is not appreciated; every chance given must be repaid tenfold.

At fifteen, though I worked hard and never complained, I had nothing to give, nothing to barter, or so I thought. We were in Samarkand, in Uzbekistan, where the people have dark, almond-shaped eyes and olive skin. After we had erected the tents and everything was ready for the evening show I was summoned to appear in the circus owner's caravan.

The owner was a huge man, a Georgian, with an enormous belly and waxed moustaches like my old dancing master, and he was totally bald. Despite his fatness, his power was awesome and he would still occasionally appear in leopard-skin tights as the circus strong man. I had heard that he could eat half a goat on his own.

I stood in front of him in bare feet and rags as he slowly peeled an orange with his thumbnail. This nail was at least five centimetres long and I had heard that it was as sharp as a razor. All the acrobats and the clowns, or anyone whom he thought was not performing properly, knew what it felt like to have his thumbnail jabbed into their backsides until the blood ran. He rotated the brilliant orange orb around his nail and I watched as the peel came away in a long circular snake. This process seemed to take a long time and when it was complete and the bright twist lay finally on the table in front of him he looked up. He had blue eyes, hooded like a reptile's, and the blue slits were so icy that you felt goosebumps when he looked at you. I had not spoken to him since he had taken all my money nearly two years before.

'What is your name, child?' he asked.

'Tamara Polyansky, sir,' I stammered, not in the least surprised that he had forgotten.

'Oh yes, the child from Omsk.' His eyes seemed to travel all over my body, then back to me. 'You want to be an acrobat, and work on the trapeze?'

'Yes, sir.' I could hardly breathe and my heart started to pound in my breast but I dared not look at him.

'Are you one of us, now?'

He meant, was I circus folk? I nodded. 'I want nothing else, sir,' I managed to whisper.

'Good,' he said. 'You may join the acrobatic troupe. Mitya Pimenov will look after you, she will be your mother.'

'Mother' is a term used in the circus which bears no relationship to the true meaning of the word. There is no mother love involved and no mothering. It meant that, in return for being trained, I would be a slave to Mitya Pimenov. She could ask me to do anything and I had no right of refusal.

But Mitya Pimenov could tumble and fly like an angel and her courage on the trapeze knew no limits. I worshipped her from afar because she was also very beautiful. But I knew enough about the training to know that she would be remorseless with me and never show me the least hint of kindness.

Female acrobats are bred to be hard. Most die young or lose a partner on the high wire or trapeze. To feel for someone and then lose them is cause for an inconsolable grief which brings with it a fear of flying. High flyers believe that the ghost of the loved one rides the wire. There is even a name given for this departed loved one, male or female: the Witch on the Wire. The superstition is that the loved one will bring about the demise of the one left behind so that they may be together again.

'Thank you, sir. I am very grateful.' My eyes cast downwards.

There was now a brittle silence between us. Finally the huge man said, 'Look up, girl! A trapeze artist is proud, unafraid, even of the circus owner. Look up, Tamara Polyansky, and watch and listen and you will learn something.'

I looked up into those terrible, cold eyes. He was holding the orange and had his thumb poised at the top of the peeled fruit. 'There is an entrance fee,' he said and his thumb pushed into the top of the orange and then rose again with a sucking sound and was pushed down once more so that some of the juice from within poured out and over the sides of the orange and onto the surface of the table. He dabbed the pudgy forefinger of his free hand into the liquid and brought it to his mouth. 'The circus owner always gets first taste, Tamara Polyansky. It is a tradition, a circus tradition.' His thumb bore down into the orange and suddenly the fruit broke open into two halves. 'What was closed must be opened. If you wish to fly like a bird we must first open the door of the cage.' He put his thumb with the sharp nail into his mouth and sucked the juice from it. 'And that is my job, I am the cage opener and I also own the bird within it.'

Tamara shrugs. 'At fifteen I became an acrobat and ...' She pauses for a moment, then says in a whisper, 'Also not a virgin any more.'

As Tamara has been speaking she has been systematically unbraiding her hair. I do not think she is conscious of doing this, it is simply a nervous gesture. But now it hangs in a shower of gold on either side of her pretty face.

She brings both her hands up and sweeps the hair back, tossing her head. 'I didn't care, I was an acrobat. In my mind I had always been an acrobat, the little rich girl was long dead. I now cared about three things only: to walk the wire, to become a trapeze artist, and to find Eugene Wilenski.

'There is not much more to tell of my circus career in the years that followed. The broken bones, the disappointment, the grinding routines, the constant striving for perfection. Trapeze artists grow old young in a circus. But I became, in circus terms, a Master of the Art, a flying trapeze artist and wire walker who could claim top billing on the circus posters.

TAMARA POLYANSKY

THE QUEEN OF HEAVEN

challenges

THE PRINCE OF DARKNESS

to a contest in which
one of them must

DIE!

'I was dressed as an angel in a brilliant blue and white leotard costume ablaze with silver spangles, all of which showed my figure to perfection. My male counterpart wore jet-black tights and top, a close-fitting cap with red horns protruding from it, and a fiery red, arrow-pointed tip on the end of his long tail.

'We would fly through the air as though in mortal combat, twisting and tumbling and catching each other. And then, when it looked certain that the Prince of Darkness would triumph, I would climb down the trapeze pole to where the high wire stretched and start across it as though escaping. The Prince of Darkness, to a dramatic drum roll, would swing across the circus tent and come down onto the wire at the opposite end, clutching a fiery sword. As he moved towards me the lights would dim to a single spotlight which transfixed the battle between good and evil on the wire.

'I would attempt to walk backwards to escape the flaming sword. I'd pretend that it was hardly possible, giving the audience the impression that I was not good on the wire and was in imminent danger of plummeting to my death.

'The audience could see that no net was strung beneath us. The dark demon with the flaming sword, catlike on the wire, came nearer and nearer until we reached the centre of the wire, thirty metres above the ring, and the spotlight went out.

'Now only the flames from the sword lit the scene and the remainder of the circus was in inky shadow. The Prince of Darkness crouched low and lunged forward, intending to run me through with his fiery blade.

'Whereupon I leapt high and catapulted over his body. The sword thrust into thin air and threw the devil completely off balance so that he plunged, sword in hand, screaming into the pitch darkness below. The orchestra stopped mid-note, and the thud of the devil's body was plainly heard as it hit the ground.

'The fiery blade had extinguished itself on the way down and now the audience waited in total darkness. Moments later a spotlight came on to reveal the devil lying in a pool of blood in the middle of the ring, impaled on his own sword.

'Then, to the haunting strains of a lone violin, the spotlight lifted to show me balanced on the wire high above. The Queen of Heaven triumphant over the Prince of Darkness. The music swelled to a glorious climax and the spotlight widened, then the orchestra died down until there was only the sound of a muffled drum as the clowns, dressed in black and wearing top hats tall as stove-pipes, carried the devil's lifeless body from the ring.'

We all spontaneously applaud, that is except the professor.

'Trick lighting, smoke and mirrors!' he says gruffly.

Tamara Polyansky grins. 'Some of it, yes. But not the leap over the devil's back. This part of the act required me to jump in the dark and land back on the wire. Though the acrobatics and wire work in the act were truly marvellous, it was this daredevil ability alone which gave me the coveted title, Master of the Art, and also, by the way, cost me thousands of hours to perfect, not to mention the broken bones and bruises!'

Tamara now has us completely in her thrall. So we are all disappointed when she says, 'Enough of circus. I was at the top of my profession and we played all over Russia. It was in St Petersburg, where the usual poster with my face on it was pasted everywhere, that I finally caught up with my mother.' She continues.

She visited me one afternoon at the circus dressed to the nines and wearing a sable fur. She coldly informed me that my father had died of the English influenza and that she had taken over his business. If she expected me to cry she was disappointed, I had given up crying a long time ago and I would grieve for my darling papa in my own way and at some other time.

'No more silly fur trading, we now deal exclusively in wool, and supply both the Russian Imperial Army and the Tsar's navy with overcoats,' she said smugly.

'Papa is dead, so who is we?' I asked.

Then she told me that she was married to a count who was also an admiral in the navy. They were in St Petersburg to receive his commission from the Tsar to be the admiral responsible for the fleet in Port Arthur. This was where a good part of the Russian fleet stood ready to defend the Tsar's dominion over Manchuria, the vast territory Russia had recently confiscated from China.

My mother seemed to relish the meeting between us and lost no time pointing out to me that she had achieved for herself what she had always hoped for her daughter and was now a countess in her own right.

She also took some delight in informing me that she had finally persuaded my father I was dead, and therefore he had left me no inheritance. Furthermore, she was now so well accustomed to the idea of my permanent demise that she felt it was much better to leave things as they were.

I remember her last words to me as she departed. 'There is no more room in my life for a clown like your father or a circus acrobat like his daughter. Goodbye, Tamara, I doubt that we shall meet again.'

So, that was that, the circus became my only family.

You will, of course, know that the Japanese attacked the Russian fleet at Port Arthur so as to take Manchuria from us. Well, on the night of the terrible attack in which most of the Russian fleet was destroyed – with thousands of casualties, among them my mother's husband the admiral – it so happened that the circus was also in Port Arthur, and by morning we found ourselves prisoners of the imperial Japanese forces.

I cannot say why the Imperial Japanese Army wanted a Russian circus, but they did.

They made us pack up and we travelled together with a long line of prisoners-of-war into Manchuria. We were treated well enough at first, and the Japanese soldiers for whom we performed nightly seemed to enjoy our show as much as their Russian counterparts. Soldiers have always liked a circus.

Circus folk will do almost anything for applause and so we soon overcame our discomfort about consorting with the enemy. After all, any audience is good when it laughs and cries and comes back for more. My angel-versus-the-devil highlight was reworked into a form the Japanese soldiers could understand and was just as successful as ever. My final leap on the wire would leave the hard-bitten soldiers swooning and gasping and at every performance dozens would faint. I suppose they were only young peasant boys really, and they would clap and cheer at the death of the Prince of Darkness who had been transformed in the Japanese version into a wicked demon.

But one night, a soldier became so carried away that he ran from his seat to where my partner lay in the centre of the ring with the sword through his body pretending to be dead, and fixing a bayonet to his rifle he repeatedly stabbed the 'dead' body through the heart before he could be pulled away.

Before I go on, I have to make a terrible confession. I had become the mistress of Colonel Tanaka, the Japanese commandant of the prisoner-of-war camp. I beg you to understand I had no choice, the circus owner was told that it was the circus or me. Naturally, I was forced to accept; the circus was my family and one does not kill one's own family, even though I would gladly have died rather than become the concubine of a Japanese officer.

I was allowed to stay with the circus and perform. The circus people knew I was keeping them all alive and so they never mentioned the liaison and were always kind to me. This had happened some time before my partner on the wire was killed by the over-excited soldier.

When my partner died I devised a solo act, but it was not the same. Japanese soldiers far and wide had heard of the Good Spirit Angel Wrestling in the Air with the Bad Spirit Demon. There was hardly a soldier in the Emperor's Imperial Japanese

Army stationed in Manchuria who would not have given a week's wages to see the original act. I was famous and, for an Occidental, much admired. The Japanese have a great capacity for theatre and make-believe and have an intense love of fantasy. According to Colonel Tanaka, the poor soldiers were all very superstitious and believed implicitly in good and evil spirits.

One morning, Colonel Tanaka rose from the tatami mat where he had made love to me and said that I would have a new circus partner. I had one month to train him to perform my signature act. As I laced up his boots he announced, 'You will be perfect in one month! If not, we stop circus and you all die!' He pointed a stubby finger at me and grinned. 'Not you, you mine! All others die! Understand?' He spoke to me in French, which was the language we used. He had learned it while studying to be an engineer in Paris.

'Master, your humble servant cannot take just anyone and train him to be an acrobat and walk the high wire. Not in a month, not even in a year!'

'He is already trained. One month, no more!' he shouted. 'He is Russian captain!'

Later that morning I was summoned by the circus owner, who, since subsisting on a meagre rice diet, had lost a considerable amount of weight and looked much the better for it. I entered his tent to find that a Russian prisoner of war stood nearby. The man had his back to me, but I could see that what remained of his uniform was in rags. He wore no boots on his feet, though the insignia on his tattered coat sleeve denoted that he was a captain in the imperial horse brigade.

'You know of this plan to give you a new partner, Tamara?' The circus owner spread his hands and sighed.

'But it's not possible! I tell you, it can't be done!' I stormed. 'This act took over two years to perfect! No man, not even God's only son, could learn it in one month!'

'I don't know about that. *He* could walk on water, Tamara Polyansky,' came the voice from the man in rags. He turned and I found myself staring into the emaciated face of Eugene Wilenski! He reached out and with the back of his index finger lightly brushed my cheek. 'Keep practising, *moy mecha,* and one day we will meet on the high wire, and then go to the trapeze where we will fly into each other's arms.'

Of the next month, what can I say? I have never worked so hard in my life. Eugene was a natural but he was rusty and, besides, he was half starved. At least I was able to get the colonel to put him on a good diet and he ate voraciously to gain the strength he needed to survive the muscular pain and falls that came with learning the act.

The first performance was nothing to shout about, but we muddled through it and the Japanese soldiers seemed not to see the many glaring imperfections in the act. But in six months we were nearly perfect. Eugene was a marvel and as I flew nightly into his arms, high above the cheering soldiers, I fell more and more deeply in love. I had always loved only him but now my whole body and soul ached to have him. At night when I lay with the colonel I imagined it was Eugene, and fantasised that we had escaped and would be passionate lovers forever until eventually we would die in each other's arms.

Once Eugene Wilenski no longer saw me as a child he began to love me too, although slowly at first. There was so little time to be kind and he had so much to learn. I was often forced to be stern, even to shout at him. Russian men, especially men from the Crimea, do not like their women to be assertive. But in the end I do not believe he could help himself and he declared his love for me.

We could never consummate our love, for if it was discovered we would both be executed. I also learned that Colonel Tanaka had found Eugene by promising that any Russian prisoner of war who came forward as a trapeze artist would save the life of another prisoner of war with every act he completed in the circus.

It was, of course, a long shot on the colonel's part, but it worked. Every day five Russian prisoners were selected at random by the colonel and executed as a matter of routine. It was called the Lottery of the Dead. Now there was this seemingly miraculous chance to save one of the lottery 'winners' each day, and so Eugene had stepped up. Our act literally became a matter of life or death. And so if we were discovered to be lovers a great many Russian prisoners would die as a consequence.

We worked together for a year and three days. Despite the

circumstances, I must tell you they were the happiest days of my life. To be so loved that every nerve end in one's body responds, this is like being in the presence of the angels. Heaven could not be a happier place.

I would fly through the air and we would do more and more figurations until, I do believe, Eugene and I were the finest aerial act in the world. And always as we performed and my body twisted with his own in the air, we were making love, fantastic love. When I felt myself grasped in his strong arms, no consummation between two lovers could have satisfied more. We made glorious love in the air and below us the Japanese soldiers were entranced by what they regarded as the eternal battle between good and evil.

When, in the end, I leapt over Eugene's lunging body and flaming sword and stood high on the wire to look down at him spotlighted in the ring, lying in a pool of fake blood with the sword seemingly thrust through his back, all I saw was a beautiful lover, exhausted from making love to me in the air and on the heavenly wire.

On the evening of the fourth day of the second year that Eugene and I were together, our act commenced as usual as the grand finale to the circus performance. That night, as Colonel Tanaka was in attendance, I dedicated our performance to him. I stood high up on the trapeze and made the dedication in Japanese, for by now I had a reasonable grasp of the language.

My enemy lover rose from his seat amongst the other officers and formally saluted. He was in his dress uniform with shining knee boots and he wore a dress sword as well as his service revolver. He seemed very pleased as he bowed then looked up at me, and I bowed in return from the trapeze high above his head. The troops all cheered their heads off and we were off to a grand start.

I knew that the dedication had been a popular success and that Colonel Tanaka had gained great face. I could sense Eugene's amusement as he stood in the dark on the trapeze platform at the other side of the tent, no doubt grinning to himself and hopeful that my gesture of respect might save more lives. I had promised him that if the colonel was pleased with the show I would attempt to persuade him to save all the next morning's lottery winners as a gesture of goodwill.

Our performance that night was perhaps more brilliant than it had ever been. We had reached the finale on the wire. Now Eugene, flaming sword in hand, advanced towards me and I, with feigned uncertainty, attempted to walk backwards on the wire to escape him. Eugene stalked me with a panther-like ease, the spotlight bringing us closer and closer, the tension building. Then, at the precise moment of the sword thrust, the scene lit only by the flames from the moving sword, a single shot rang out.

In the light cast by the flaming sword I saw a brilliant scarlet spray of blood as a bullet ripped open Eugene's chest and he fell backwards away from me and then plunged wildly downwards, but not in the prescribed arc so that he could be caught in a small net positioned in the darkness. I instinctively jumped as he fell from the wire and the circus tent went into total darkness. I landed back on the wire in the dark and held my balance, my heart beating furiously as I heard a scream rising in my throat. When it came I didn't seem to hear it, so deafening was the pounding in my ears. Moments later the spotlight came back on, but Eugene did not lie in his accustomed spot in the centre of the circus ring, though I could clearly see the pool of fake blood prepared for his body. The spotlight swayed, then moved left and then right and forward again across the ring until it found his broken body and held still.

The Japanese soldiers were yelling and screaming their heads off, thinking it was all a part of the act. Suddenly Colonel Tanaka walked into the spotlight and stood beside Eugene's broken body. Slowly he drew his samurai sword, holding its lacquered haft in both hands, then with a fierce, sharp shout he raised the samurai sword above his head and swiftly brought it down, the blade whipping in the air before separating Eugene's head from his body.

There is a gasp and then a soft moan to my left and Olga Zorbatov slumps beside me into a dead faint. Anya and Sophia Shebaldin both have their hands up to their faces and Mr Mendelsohn breaks down and weeps. For my part, while I am deeply shocked, I have seen the Cossacks do much the same thing in my village and I am probably the first to compose myself.

Tamara is now weeping loudly and I rise and take her into my arms. 'Sshhh! We will help you, we are your friends, Tamara,' I say, rocking her like a baby. It is not much, but soon her tears stop and she quietens. After some time she looks up and draws herself away from me and needlessly apologises to us all.

In the meantime we have all forgotten about poor Olga Zorbatov, but, like a true Taurus, she gives a sudden bellow and promptly recovers from her faint. To be born under the sign of the Bull is not easy; nobody seems in the least concerned for her.

'It is enough for one night,' I say.

But Tamara's hand rises to still me. 'No, please, Mrs Moses, I do not possess the strength to go through this again another night. With your kind permission I would like to complete my story.'

So Tamara Polyansky tells us how Colonel Tanaka discovered her love for Eugene.

The circus owner was invited to a reception by some visiting Japanese officers after a circus performance. Drunk and hoping to ingratiate himself, he had whispered into the ear of an infantry captain that the two high-flying trapeze artists were lovers. The captain, thinking little of this information, mentioned it in passing to another officer, and eventually Colonel Tanaka came to hear of it.

On that dreadful night, Colonel Tanaka waited for me to come down from the high wire and then dragged me by the hair towards the owner's tent.

'You have been unfaithful!' he screamed in Japanese. 'You must pay with your life, whore!'

'Kill me! I beg you to kill me!' I shouted back. 'Do it now, shoot me now!' I sobbed.

Instead, Tanaka threw me inside the tent where the circus owner cowered in the corner on his knees. His former flab was by now reduced to folds of skin which hung down like curtain drapes. He crawled whimpering on his knees towards Colonel Tanaka and commenced to beg for mercy, sobbing and then kissing the toes of his highly polished dress boots.

Tanaka released his grip on my hair and I fell to the ground but then leapt up again. 'Kill me, you bastard!' I screamed, attacking him with my nails. Tanaka knocked me down with the back of his hand, but I rose again just as he drew his revolver and shot the circus owner through the back of the head.

'You!' he snarled in French to me. 'For you something worse than death!'

I was sent to northern Japan where I became a comfort woman in a brothel for Japanese soldiers. Here I would often be used a hundred times a day. If I had not been constantly watched I would have taken my own life a dozen times. Then, in 1910, when a small earthquake disrupted the brothel and the guards were seen running for their lives, I escaped. I eventually found my way across the La Perouse Strait to the Russian island of Sakhalin where I told my story to the military authorities.

But I found little comfort from my own people. Instead, I was informed that I was wanted by the Third Section, the Tsar's secret police, as well as the military authorities. The military said they wanted me for consorting with the enemy and the Third Section for being a spy against imperial Russia.

Because the secret police had precedence over the military, and was besides a huge and somewhat befuddled bureaucracy, it was somehow necessary for me to be interrogated in Moscow several thousand kilometres away. The military declared that they would gladly save the Tsar the expense and simply take me out and shoot me, and afterwards send Moscow a bill for the cost of one bullet wasted on the little yellow man's whore.

I will spare you a description of my journey, first by boat and then by train across Russia. There are few miseries as great. But after several weeks, when it became apparent that I had no interest in escaping and didn't care whether I lived or died, my guards removed the shackles from my wrists and ankles so that I could prepare their food and do other duties, including the one I had been doing for the Japanese soldiers. The uniforms may change, but what's below the belt of a man who has power over a woman remains constant.

We were in the final stages of our journey to Moscow and I had long reconciled myself to the fact that I was going to die. In a perverse sort of way, I welcomed the fact that the Third Section would make my death a long and painful one.

I did not believe I had a right to live. Too many people had died because of me. Eugene, all the circus folk, and hundreds of prisoners of war who might otherwise have been saved if I had not loved Eugene so much.

We were perhaps a day's journey from Moscow and it was late at night when we came to a halt at the tiny railroad station with the name of Astapovo. It was so small and remote that my guards allowed me to alight so that I might fetch fresh water and wash out the samovar in which I brewed their tea.

It was cold, late autumn, November-cold, when the wind starts to blow in from the north. I wore only a threadbare kapok coat over a coarse linen dress and on my feet peasant sandals made of hemp. I entered the small shack on the platform from which came a dim light. I thought I might enquire about water, most railway stations had a well close by. In the corner, lit by a tiny oil lamp of the kind a traveller might use, lay a frail old man gasping and wheezing. Beside him was a small suitcase and a large vacuum flask, which I hoped might contain something warm to drink. I was beyond caring that the old man seemed to be dying. I had seen so much death, if anything I felt that since his time appeared to be just about up, he had no further use for the flask beside him.

I slowly approached him and stretched my hand out to take the flask. I was close enough to touch him. My hand paused, leaving the flask where it stood. The old man was Leo Tolstoy, the great writer.

I knew this with absolute certainty. The misshapen nose, high brow, bald head, his piercing blue eyes now somewhat dimmed, and, of course, the great white beard. What convinced me though was the sable coat he wore. Old peasant men do not die in sable coats. It was the coat my father had given him. I knew it was Tolstoy as sure as I knew the nose on my own face.

I lifted him into my arms; he was surprisingly light and even through the lustrous fur coat I could feel his sharp old bones.

'Count Tolstoy, I would consider it a great honour if you would let me help you,' I heard myself saying in the accent of my former well-bred self.

'Child, I am dying, there is nothing you can do for me but report it to the authorities.' He seemed to smile and then continued, 'Who, I feel sure, will report it to the Tsar and to the Church. Both will be pleasantly surprised to hear the good news of my demise and will perhaps call for some positive verification – a lock from my beard, perhaps, or a finger for a future *reliquiae* of the devil himself?'

'I met you at my tenth birthday party, Master. You came to our house to ...' I stopped. 'Well, I'm not at all sure I know why you came.'

For a moment a gleam came into his eyes. 'Ah, the birthday girl who wanted to be an acrobat. How did it go?'

'It went not so well, sir. I go to Moscow where the Tsar would have me killed.' I shrugged. 'It matters little to me, my life is finished.'

'No, my child, your life is hardly begun. Never let them get the better of you. Not until your final breath. Never give up! Damn the Tsar, damn his eyes and his soul, may he rest in an unmarked grave! Child, leave Russia and only return when the Tsar and those like him have been overthrown.' With these strange words he slumped back in my arms.

I let him down gently and rushed out of the small hut. 'It's Tolstoy, Count Leo Tolstoy, he is dying in there!' I cried.

Of course, at first, the people on the train thought I had gone crazy. But I kept running up and down and yelling until a reluctant train inspector alighted, and then another official followed him and then, when they entered the hut and didn't immediately return, more people crowded around until every passenger had spilled out onto the tiny platform and beyond. Someone with more credibility than I positively indentified Tolstoy, no doubt having seen his picture, or perhaps from the contents of his small suitcase. As I remember, there were almost as many pictures of him in Russia as there were of Tsar Nicholas. And, of course, there was the sable coat.

'It is Tolstoy, he is dying!' people were shouting and running around. They were shocked but also secretly consumed by excitement and pride, though trying not to show it. They knew they were eyewitnesses to history, to a national tragedy, news that would shake Russia to the core and spread like a whirlwind around the world.

It was then that I quietly slipped into the night. I had just taken advice from the greatest intellect Russia had ever produced, a man acknowledged by all Russians to be the greatest writer in literature. If he said I was not yet ready to surrender, who was I to argue?

And then one day I found Mrs Moses, who will lead us through the wilderness to the promised land.

News of Tolstoy's collapse in the obscure railroad station of Astapovo, one hundred and sixty kilometres to the south-east of Moscow, was spread along telegraph wires throughout Russia and the world. After he was discovered he lay dying for several days in the little railway station, finally passing away on the 26th of September 1910, with the world's newsreel photographers recording his death. He refused absolution from the Church or visits from representatives of the Tsar, and would not even see his wife with whom he had quarrelled incessantly to the very end.

1 cup/185 g/6½ oz mixed dried fruit

½ cup/110 g/4 oz mixed citrus peel

1 tablespoon glacé cherries

2 tablespoons brandy

½ cup/125 g/4 oz butter

½ cup/125 g/4 oz dark brown sugar

3 eggs

1 cup/140 g/5 oz plain flour

½ teaspoon bicarbonate of soda

1 teaspoon mixed spice

¼ cup/40 g/1½ oz blanched **almonds**, roughly chopped

Fancy POLYANSKY Plum Pudding

Butter a 1 litre pudding basin and line the bottom with baking paper. Cut out another disk of baking paper for the top of the pudding.

Combine the dried fruit, mixed peel and cherries in a large bowl and add the brandy. Leave to soak for 3 to 4 hours or overnight.

Cream the butter and sugar until smooth, then add the eggs, one at a time, mixing well between each addition.

Sift together the flour, bicarbonate of soda and mixed spice. Fold into the creamed mixture alternately with the fruits, adding any remaining liquid. Fold the almonds through the mixture.

Spoon the pudding into the basin and cover the top with baking paper. Cover the top of the basin with a double layer of aluminium foil, tied securely around the basin with string.

Bring some water to the boil in a large saucepan. Lower the basin into the saucepan – the water should come two-thirds of the way up the sides. Cover the saucepan and keep the water boiling while steaming. Top up with boiling water from the kettle as necessary.

Boil for 3 to 4 hours until cooked through (test with a skewer). Turn out, remove the baking paper, and serve with hot custard.

Serves 4 to 6

Cleopatra's
CAT
and the Letters from
EGYPT

WHAT CAN I TELL YOU ABOUT MRS SHEBALDIN? SHE

is a newcomer, a recent addition to our little half-starved journey into freedom. There is not much required to join us, we ask few questions and are not concerned with religion.

Jew, Christian, Muslim – it is all the same, because when you are hungry and frightened the God you choose is important only to yourself. The prerequisite for travelling with us is that you must be able to walk. So when Mrs Shebaldin told us that she was a foot doctor we ceased immediately to be curious; never mind the fancy questions, a foot doctor is a gift from whatever loving God.

Like the professor who never completed the journey to Siberia, and Tamara who sent herself there, Sophia Shebaldin also has a story to tell of the desolate wasteland with the name that comes cold and dead to the lips.

It is necessary before Mrs Shebaldin tells her story to speak of Siberia so that we may understand where her husband was sent and how he would have suffered his long incarceration. She has not been there but the professor and Tamara have and it is their description and an incident once told to us by the professor that paints the picture of this desolate landscape.

Siberia, if you say it slowly, is a malicious word, like a blunt knife pushed slowly into the stomach. It is a landscape filled with dread, a howling gale in the Russian imagination. It is the foul breath of the universe, an endless stench of dark landscape and permafrost where there is no joy, no warm blood, nor kind earth or sun for the spawning of happiness.

Siberia is where the air itself is the prison guard. It has long been the place the Tsars have sent Russia's so-called enemies, the land where the secret police bury their victims alive in the remorseless tundra and so turn good strong men into the walking dead.

When a judge condemns a man to Siberia it is not unusual to allow him first to return to his village to attend his own funeral and get drunk at his wake. The judge knows that the Gulag is a one-way trip and every man is entitled to say farewell to his family and kiss his own life a fond goodbye.

In Siberia, the gates of the slave camps stay open. Only a minimum of guards are required and fewer still in the salt mines. These are dull men who will beat you senseless if you don't work but will invite you to leave any time you may care to do so. 'Be my guest. Tonight? But of course! You've had enough? Well done! Freedom? Certainly, let me show you to the front gate.' They will turn to the slave next to you. 'This is your lucky day, my friend. Tonight you shall have his tin of tepid water which carries the grand name of soup.'

To escape in Siberia is to die alone and there is nothing a person fears more than that his exit from life will take place unremarked. It is unbearable for a man to think of his spirit rising into the screeching wind, sucked up into the midnight maw of uncaring space without receiving a benediction and making his confession with the last of his breath.

A man has every right to fear that his soul will lose its way in the vast loneliness, that the howling of the *dybbuk*, his ghost, will be added to the fury of the winter gales. Who will wait with you so that he might cover your silent mouth and close your eyes, at the same time stealing the gold ring from your finger as a keepsake, a small mark of your passing?

The professor tells of his journey to Siberia. He is on his way to the salt mines, thirty men in a cattle truck, a hundred trucks transporting three thousand prisoners. The only sound day after day the clickity-clack of the wheels and the puff and huff and labour of the hot black engine half a kilometre ahead.

After a week, the men who huddle together against the bitter cold seldom talk. The conversation between them is long exhausted; lives have been explained, laid bare, similarities explored, experiences shared, coincidences examined, connections made, alliances considered. All this and more, until the bones of past relationships have been picked white and discarded. It is now every man for himself as compassion and hope die in the breasts of each of them.

Now there is only the rock and sway of the cattle trucks and the click and clack of steel wheels beneath their feet. They yearn for a little comfort and put great store in the added warmth to be gained from huddling together against the biting cold. Occasionally a fight breaks out, a pathetic squabble, like two stray dogs over an old bone as one prisoner tries to snatch a warmer place from a weaker man who may be fortunate enough to lay his cheek against someone who wears a fur coat or a collar of silver fox.

The train stops for twenty minutes every two days to take on water and coal. It is usually snowing and the temperature is below freezing, minus thirty, maybe even more. The engine grinds to a halt, a screaming and whining of metal on frozen rails and a fuss of escaping piston steam. The door to the trucks are opened and prisoners are let out to defecate.

The professor continues his story and he apologises for the coarse language he feels he must use, explaining that to use words other than piss and shit would alter the sense of what happened.

We nod for him to continue. He is not a man with a dirty mouth and is easily the most educated amongst us; besides, these not-so-nice words we all know exist and so we nod the go-ahead, accepting a suspension of good manners as a necessity for an honest telling of the story.

But, of course, Olga Zorbatov brings her finger and thumb to clasp her nose, the usual exception to our accord.

'The men learn quickly that when you piss you do not remove your trousers. You simply micturate where you stand, the warm urine running down the inside of your trouser legs. Remove your trousers and the piss freezes in the air, an arc of golden ice that drills back and stabs into the urethra, the penis, the pain of which is said to be indescribable.

'To defecate is not so bad, the trousers may be lowered if the hands are cupped tightly over the genitals to keep them warm. The buttocks may start to freeze but they contain sufficient fat to protect them and the faecal matter within will still drop and the trousers be restored in time.'

I now see why the professor has to use common words, after all, the ones he uses to replace them, micturate and faecal material, are most complicated and don't sound a bit like what people do, you know, when they have to go.

'By the time the cattle trucks have been opened the men have about ten minutes to do their business. Both sides of the railway lines are beaded with hundreds of men squatting with their trousers around their ankles. A few have walked away from the side of the trucks, mostly city folk of the better class who are too modest to do their business in public.

'The whistle blows and the train immediately starts to move away, there are only moments left to scramble back into the trucks. Most of the men make it, but those who have strayed from the line are seen frantically running to reach their own truck, calling out desperately. They are urged on by the calls of their comrades who have their hands stretched out to help them aboard, for if they miss boarding the truck to which they belong no other will take them on board.

'But now comes the cruel joke. Those who are too modest to squat beside the rail are also generally the ones who are too shy to clasp their genitals in public. The genitals are the warmest place on the body and when your hands are closed around the scrotum your fingers are prevented from freezing. Now as the train pulls away they rise, only to discover that their hands are frozen and they cannot pull their trousers up. So they struggle to hold them up with the sides of their arms while they run, but when they stretch their hands out to be helped aboard, the trousers drop to their ankles and they trip, ploughing into the dirty snow beside the track. There is only hapless laughter from those safely aboard. A man running after a departing train with his trousers falling slowly down around his ankles is very funny even if it is also terribly sad. Tragedy and laughter are twin brothers in Siberia.

'With the mirth of his comrades ringing in his ears a man will pick himself up, but by now the engine is gaining speed and so he stands bare-arsed in the snow helplessly watching his own life disappearing from sight.

'At each coaling stop half a dozen men are left to die in the wind and the blinding snow, a black smudge of engine smoke against the pewter-coloured sky their last tenuous connection with the living. Good friends; the milch cows coming into the village at sundown; the sharp cries of mothers scolding their children; hot soup; the sound of laughter from a lighted tavern; the memory of a first, late-summer mating with a blue-eyed, flaxen-haired maiden in a rustling cornfield; the mewling of a newborn infant – lost forever in the smoke that slowly spreads and fades against the eyeless horizon.'

The professor looks up and opens his hands wide and sighs. 'What more can I say? That is the train to Siberia.'

Mrs Shebaldin looks up and also sighs, then she says, 'I have spent the last five years of my life in Siberia but I too have never been there. I have been living in Egypt.'

For riddles we haven't got time, I think to myself. Whatever does she mean?

'My husband was a doctor, a famous surgeon,' Mrs Shebaldin goes on to explain. 'We lived in a fine house in St Petersburg near the Academy of Medicine in the Nevsky Prospekt. Uri was a modernist, a Deep Knife, which is what they called the younger surgeons at the academy. The older ones had no interest in what lay under the skin but only in what they could see to chop off.

'"Why leave in what is harmful and will do further harm when it may be neatly cut out and stitched?" my husband would say. "An ulcer will not cure itself nor, for the most part, will an abscess on the bowel drain away." He was also a confirmed follower of Charles Darwin. "Nature doesn't always take care of the redundant pieces, we evolve and change but so slowly that there are parts of the human physiology which have become unnecessary. When these give trouble they must be removed."'

'Which parts are those, Madam Shebaldin?' the professor asks.

'Professor, I am not a scientist like you, but my husband talked in particular of the tonsils and the appendix,' Mrs Shebaldin says, and then to our surprise she suddenly bursts into tears.

'Whatever have I said to upset you, Madam?' the professor cries in alarm.

'Not you, Professor,' Sophia Shebaldin sniffs. 'It is the thought of an appendectomy. The first appendectomy operation to be performed in Russia, it was the cause of my tragedy, our eventual downfall!'

She is not the crying type. Sophia Shebaldin is a thin woman who seems to be composed of sharp edges and hard flat places. Narrow-chested, high-shouldered, legs like knotted twigs on tiny feet, skin stretched taut over her face, a reserved person who does not encourage familiarity, though her expression is never unwelcoming. There is simply no fuss to her. Even her grey hair is smoothed and pulled so tightly back into a bun that it gives less the impression of hair than of a helmet fashioned in steel. And her hands are long and thin, but not beautiful like Mr

Mendelsohn's. It is as though her fingers and palms contain no flesh, only a layer of skin to hide the bones beneath.

It is only when she massages your tired feet, or works on a painful corn or drains a blister or gently rubs a sprained ankle, that you know immediately these are special hands, the hands of a true healer. She lays them on a painful place and those long, bony fingers seem to flush out the pain, making it disappear into thin air. They seem to pluck it out of the muscle or the bruise, as though indignant that it should be there at all. In an hour or two you are ready for the road again.

Sophia looks up at the professor as she speaks. 'You will perhaps recall that the English king, Edward the Seventh, who is cousin to Tsar Nicholas, received the first operation on the human appendix the very day before his coronation was to take place. It was a desperate measure by the royal surgeon Sir Frederick Treves, and it saved the king's life.'

The professor nods, though I am not sure that like the rest of us this is not news to him as well. Russia and England are not friends at the moment and not much is heard about the English people that is complimentary. For my part I am not even sure what is this appendix that nearly killed the English king?

'Not so fast if you please, Sophia,' I say. 'What is this appendectomy when it's at home?'

'Just a little wormlike thing located on the lower right of the stomach,' she says, touching a spot on her lower abdomen.

'A little worm that's blind and does nothing, so what's the problem please?' Olga Zorbatov asks again.

Sophia looks at Mrs Z. 'The problem is, this little worm can become infected and cause inflammation and terrible pain and even burst, and a person with appendicitis may die,' Sophia says. 'They were trying to drain the infection from the English king but the pain and the cramps grew more severe and on the night before his coronation, fever, vomiting and diarrhoea threatened to kill him. The surgeon decided to open him up and drain the infection on the spot and so history was made. Maybe it was not the first appendix operation. Who can say for sure? But it was the first on a king and so naturally everyone says it is the first on anybody. And the news spread around the world, even to Russia.'

Men are all little boys at heart, even surgeons. Uri and his colleagues at the academy hear soon enough about this kingly operation and suddenly it is appendix this and appendectomy that and appendicitis something else. Every peasant who comes along with a stomach ache they want to open up and cut out his little worm. And then one night, very late, long after we have gone to bed, comes a knock at the door of our house. It is a footman from the palace of Prince Felix Youssopov and he has a note from a physician who is well known among the nobility. It asks for Uri to come to the prince's palace at Dvortsovaya Ploshchad at once, and to bring his surgical instruments with him.

It is nearly two o'clock in the morning when Uri arrives and he is taken immediately to a bedchamber where a small girl is lying. She is maybe eight years old, and he is informed that she is the prince's favourite niece and also related to the Tsar and must be saved.

Uri goes into consultation with the physician, who is convinced that the child has appendicitis. She has a high fever, cramps in the area around the right hip bone and navel, frequent nausea and vomiting and she is in great pain. The child has been sick for several days and in the last two hours has become unconscious. The physician wants Uri to conduct an emergency operation right there in the palace. Everything has been made ready in the kitchen, surfaces have been scrubbed and disinfected, water is boiling and extra lamps have been brought in to aid the operation.

Uri is reluctant, he belongs to the new school of hygiene and the palace kitchen is not suitable for complete sterilisation. Besides, he has not personally conducted an appendectomy operation before. The little princess's pulse rate is dangerously low and he is reluctant to give her chloroform which in these conditions could quite easily have stopped her heart.

'You *must* operate!' the famous physician insists. 'This is no different to the English king. The prince will not forgive you if she dies! The Youssopov family has eighty grand estates all over Russia and is second in power only to the Tsar himself.' He fixes Uri with his monocle. 'What kind of future career do you imagine you will have at the Academy of Medicine?' He nods his head towards the unconscious child. 'That is to say, if the little princess should die without an attempt to save her? On the other hand, if the child should live, a professor of surgery is not entirely out of the question.'

Well, my Uri performed the operation but they had called him in too late, and as the infection had spread to the abdominal cavity, the princess died two days later of peritonitis. The first appendix operation performed on a royal personage in Russia had failed.

The news of the princess's death was carried by the newspapers and the comparison was naturally made with the English surgeon, Sir Frederick Treves. A great scandal was in the making, court gossips pointed out that the English king had been saved but a Russian surgeon couldn't even manage to save a small princess who belonged to minor royalty. The papers lamented that Russia, the Tsar and the powerful Youssopov family had been disgraced and humiliated. A scapegoat was needed and Uri was arrested as a clandestine Bolshevik seeking to destroy the throne and sentenced to five years in the salt mines in Siberia.

The judge allowed Uri to return home for the banquet of farewell or, as it is known by the lower orders and country people, the Feast of the Dead. An open coffin is brought by pallbearers into the prisoner's house and, at one stage during the festivities, he is made to lie in his own death box. The village priest says the prayers for the dearly departed over his live body, whereupon the guests drink a toast of vodka to his future memory.

The banquet of farewell held for Uri was a less bizarre affair, but nevertheless his colleagues from the Medical Academy, those who were not too frightened to attend, and our friends and relations scarcely harboured any more hope for his safe return than a peasant family might for a convicted son or father.

Finally the time came for Uri to bid our little family, myself and our two girls, goodbye. It was a terrible moment for we were very much in love, and Uri doted on Tanya and little Anna. The death of the princess had caused him a great deal of personal distress, the little girl had been the same age as Tanya our eldest, just seven and a half. Somehow, Uri felt himself to blame, even though both professors of surgery at the academy, called in at the autopsy, had testified that all the evidence indicated the surgeon's knife had come too late to save the child, and that peritonitis, well advanced before the incision was made, had been the certain cause of her death.

But then the sentence never was about right or wrong, neglect or otherwise. It was about Russia being made to seem inferior to the hated English. The so-called brilliant young surgeon, Uri Shebaldin, unlike the Britisher Sir Frederick Treves, was not up to scratch, or a Bolshevik, or both. It is from such childish notions that the diplomacy of nations is constructed and national pride is gained or lost.

I confess that at our final parting I shed bitter tears. Little Anna, not yet six years old, seeing my distress crawled onto her father's knee. 'Why are you leaving us, Papa?' she asked. 'Why is Mama crying so?'

Uri, barely able to contain his own grief, kissed the top of her head and then also drew Tanya to his side. 'I am going to visit the Queen of Egypt,' he said. 'She has a beautiful daughter just like you and Tanya, only her little girl has hair black as midnight and eyes the colour of jade.'

'What's her name?' Anna asked.

'Who? The Queen of Egypt or her daughter?'

'The Queen's name is Cleopatra, silly!' Tanya said to her younger sister. 'Everyone knows that!'

Anna, not to be outdone, shot back, 'I know that too, I do, I do! What's the name of her daughter, Papa?'

Uri thought for a moment. 'Princess Nefertiti,' he said with a smile.

'How long will you go away, Papa?' Tanya asked.

'Five years, my darling. You will be thirteen and Anna will be eleven, practically grown up when I return.'

'Can't you stay with us? What will become of our mother?' Anna cried.

There were tears in Uri's eyes as he held his two little daughters even closer. 'Mother Russia must come first, my darlings. She has decided I must go away.' Two tears rolled slowly down Uri's cheeks.

'Is she more important than our mother?' Tanya asked incredulously.

'She is the mother of everyone in Russia and cannot be denied,' I said, saving Uri from a reply which might upset his children. I felt that my heart would break and my lips trembled as I fought to hold back my tears.

Anna climbed from her father's knee and skipped from the room, apparently satisfied with the answer and not understanding the implications of Uri's departure. She returned a few minutes later with a small ginger kitten which she held up to her father. 'You must give it to Queen Cleopatra, Papa. It is a gift from all of us.'

Uri took the kitten, which practically disappeared in his big surgeon's hands, and put it into the pocket of his greatcoat. 'Thank you, darling.' He kissed Anna and then Tanya. 'I shall ask Cleopatra's cat to let you know how things go for us in Egypt.'

'Cats can't write letters!' Anna exclaimed.

Uri patted the pocket of his overcoat. 'I will teach this one to write, just you see.'

At that moment a captain in the Third Section who was in charge of the escorting militia entered the room. 'It is time to go, Surgeon Shebaldin.'

When, perhaps two days later, I had stopped weeping continuously for my husband, I sat quietly thinking what might become of us. Uri had always been a loving and considerate husband and a wonderful father, and the emotional burden of bringing up the two girls on my own seemed overwhelming. I tried to capture evey moment of his last few hours with us, his reassurance that he would return, that five years was not so long. Then we would leave Russia, he said, and go elsewhere to make a fresh start. It was then I thought briefly of the kitten taken by Anna from a litter in the stables, although I confess it was no more than a small detail in the tragedy of losing my husband forever. I simply assumed Uri would have given the kitten to someone, he was much too kind a man to leave it to die. Then, some weeks later, Anna came to breakfast one morning and enquired why we hadn't yet received a letter from Cleopatra's cat.

'It has been five weeks. Is Egypt so far away that Papa hasn't arrived yet? Or do you think I gave him a stupid cat, one that can't learn to write, Mama?'

Tanya sighed heavily. 'Egypt is a long way away, so they haven't even arrived yet,' she said firmly. 'Besides, you can't teach a cat to write in five weeks, silly!'

I thought for a moment that I should enlighten them, tell them the truth about their papa. But then I changed my mind, they were simply too young to face the prospect of never seeing their father again. There are, after all, many ways to handle one's personal grief and the notion of my beloved Uri arriving at the court of the Queen of Egypt on a diplomatic posting from the Tsar seemed no less improbable than the reason he was being sent to Siberia. So I allowed myself to indulge a little in the children's fantasy.

'If anyone can teach a cat to write it is your papa,' I said. 'I feel sure that we will soon have news from Cleopatra's cat, who will tell us how your darling papa is getting on.'

Anna was a persistent child and two months later she asked again why we hadn't heard from Cleopatra's cat. She pronounced it as though the two words were no longer a description but a proper name – Cleopatra's Cat.

I had written every week to Uri, sending my letter to an address he had given me, a hospital in a town in south-western Siberia nearest to where the salt mines are located. Russia, he argued, has few enough doctors and even fewer surgeons. Uri had been confident that once he arrived at his destination the authorities would put him to work in the prison hospital. Or, if no such institution existed, then in the hospital in the town nearest to the prison camp.

However, it was a logical assumption in a country where logic and commonsense play a very minor part in the behaviour of the bureaucracy. It had been four and a half months since I first wrote to him, and I had received no replies. My beloved Uri had simply disappeared from the face of the earth.

I still agonised over whether or not I should tell my children that their father would never return. The notion that the cat would write had gathered momentum, and they had become obsessed with the need to hear from it.

I too, needed the comfort of believing my husband was still alive. My two precious daughters were all I had left in life and to cause them to share my misery, though it may in the long run have proved to be a wiser thing to do, was quite beyond me at the time.

So I decided to write to my daughters in the guise of Cleopatra's Cat. I soon convinced myself that this was not as silly as it seemed. I would continue to write to Uri, but now the letters could be channelled through Cleopatra's Cat. I could reply to letters which it would seem we had received, the girls would retain some sense of their beloved father, and he would remain a significant and loving influence in their young lives.

I will give you a small, and perhaps trite, example:

Tell Papa that we know he is on a secret mission for Mother Russia and too busy to write but we love him and miss him. With all our love to him come lots of loving strokes for you, from Tanya, Anna and Sophia. Tell him never a day passes when he isn't in our thoughts.

P.S. Your brothers and sisters in the stables are practically grown up and are almost capable of earning their living catching mice, of which there are a great many after the warmer winter. What are the Egyptian mice like, do they also have fleas? Anna wants to know.

S, T & little A.

I would write long letters to the children describing the land of Egypt and life in the royal palace of Cleopatra. There were stories of expeditions on the royal barge down the Nile, all seen from a cat's viewpoint, of course. I told them that a cat in Egypt had almost the same status as a priest and that life was pretty cushy. That because I was the only ginger cat in Egypt, I was considered to be the most beautiful cat in the whole world. My best friend, naturally, was Princess Nefertiti and I told them about the exotic life of a royal princess, including all the things I wished my own little daughters to learn. I wrote that Nefertiti and I were inseparable and that Cleopatra even required me to be seated on her lap during royal occasions, wearing a collar of emeralds and rubies. The most special of these occasions was when the diplomatic corps were presented to the Queen. I added that Papa was always the one singled out by Cleopatra. He was her absolute favourite diplomat and confidante. So the two of us were bringing great honour to Mother Russia in Egyptian diplomatic circles.

I wrote of plots and conspiracies in the royal court and how I, Cleopatra's Cat, friend, seeker after the truth and brilliant spy, could travel silently and unseen over the rooftops. Under a starry midnight sky I would venture into the palaces of the foreign diplomats and overhear their intrigues and salacious gossip.

The important information I would, of course, take to Uri and the juicy bits of gossip directly to the Queen herself. Increasingly she came to depend on the Russian diplomat Uri Shebaldin to inform her of any danger to her throne, and she revelled in the bedchamber gossip I supplied, often using it to taunt a pompous ambassador.

Tanya and Anna grew terribly anxious when several of Cleopatra's Cat's letters related how diplomats from other countries began to bring the Queen of Egypt and her daughter Nefertiti cats as gifts: Siamese and Persian cats, and Manx cats with no tails, Tibetan cats with brilliant blue eyes, and Bengal felines that looked like tiny leopards. Cats with almond eyes black as Mesopotamian olives; cats with pink noses and sharply pointed ears, dark as midnight with collars of South Sea pearls. All proffered in an attempt to win the Queen's favour. But to no avail – Cleopatra's Cat won every contest with her agility, beauty and intelligence and remained the topmost cat in Egypt.

The adventures of Cleopatra's Cat and the Queen of Egypt grew more and more extravagant as I invented a new life for Uri, who through his knowledge of surgery had saved many an important Egyptian personage. I added that he was loved by the peasants who tilled the fields and sailed the graceful dhows on the Nile because he never spared himself and would operate on a camel driver or goatherd as readily as on a prince or temple priest.

I even utilised the principle reason for our tragedy and wrote a letter from Cleopatra's Cat telling how Uri saved the life of Princess Nefertiti when she burst her appendix. Naturally I invented a happy ending. Cleopatra's Cat told the girls how their father was showered with fresh honours by the Queen, and was the envy of all the foreign countries for saving the life of the beautiful young princess.

There was a story of how the British ambassador had swallowed a fish bone at a diplomatic dinner and was in danger of choking to death and how Uri had opened his throat on the spot with a meat skewer and removed the lethal bone. For this life-saving act a grateful British government had given him the title, Sir Uri Shebaldin, Surgeon to the Queen of Egypt. From that moment on, each of the letters from Cleopatra's Cat ended with the words: 'Another Cat-astrophe avoided by Sir Uri Shebaldin, Surgeon to the Queen of Egypt, the purr-fect physician!'

But little girls grow bigger every day and soon the five years Uri had promised them he would be away were almost up. I had not received a word from my husband from the day of his departure. I had written to him every week, enclosing a copy of Cleopatra's Cat's letter from Egypt and our reply, telling him of our little lives in St Petersburg and how we missed and loved him with all our hearts.

Now, with the girls demanding their father's return, I wrote a desperate letter from Cleopatra's Cat saying that so many Egyptians had been saved from certain death by the miracle of Uri's surgery that Queen Cleopatra had begged Tsar Nicholas to let him stay a while longer. The cat wrote that she was bitterly disappointed by the Tsar's agreement, which allowed Uri to remain at the Court of Egypt for a further two years.

I was playing for time but, of course, the game was up. Tanya and Anna had put pressure on me precisely so that I would come clean. In fact, for some time they had been going along with the letters, long after they suspected the truth. They understood that I needed to write the Cleopatra's Cat letters to maintain my own courage.

But sooner or later the balloon of fantasy comes down to earth. We had just completed breakfast one morning when Tanya looked up and said, 'Mama, Papa isn't coming back, is he?'

Before I could reply Anna piped up. 'He's been sent to Siberia, hasn't he?'

While I had been expecting this moment, it nevertheless came as a shock. The letters from Cleopatra's Cat, albeit from my own pen, had become such an intrinsic part of our lives that I had somehow never given up the hope that Uri would some day return to us. One morning or evening we would look up at the sound of the doorbell, and when we went to open the door there he would be. A little thinner perhaps, with grey streaks in his hair, but that old familiar grin, his big surgeon's hands dangling at his sides, and perched on his shoulder would be a big ginger cat.

Now, confronted by the truth, I looked out of the window onto the street, not knowing what to say to my two lovely daughters. I could see the postman coming down the street and, not wishing to have Tanya and Anna see me crying, I said,

'Quick, both of you, there's the postman, run and see if their isn't a letter for us from Egypt.'

'Oh Mama!' Tanya cried. 'I am so sorry to have hurt you!' But she went with Anna to meet the postman. My eyes filled with tears. Tanya came back into the parlour, followed by Anna, and both stood silently by my side as I sobbed. Then Tanya pulled a chair and Anna took me by the hand as they guided me into the chair where I sat with my elbows on the table and my face covered by my hands. I simply couldn't stop sobbing and I didn't quite know why. After all, I had always known this moment must come.

'Mama, there is a letter,' I heard Tanya saying, but it was as though her voice came to me in a fog. I realised that she had been repeating this statement for some time. Then I felt her shaking my shoulder. 'Mama, there is a letter, I think from Siberia.'

Sophia Shebaldin looks up at us. 'I swear it on my mother's grave, the letter arrived the very morning the girls finally demanded to know about their father.' Sophia Shebaldin looks as though the story might end right there, for she strokes the front of her dress as though she is about to rise.

'Please do not stop now!' Mr Mendelsohn begs. 'A letter from your husband? It is good news? He is coming back maybe, yes?'

Sophia Shebaldin smiles.

The letter was only a few words: 'Make a great feast, Cleopatra's Cat is returning home. The letter is in the bottom of the cage.' What followed was a date and the time the Trans-Siberian train came into the grand station at St Petersburg.

It was such a tiny note, but it told us everything we needed to know. Uri had received my letters, he was alive and he was coming home. What was meant by the words 'The letter is in the bottom of the cage' was impossible to tell. Though it didn't seem to matter now that we knew he was alive.

I grabbed the girls and we danced and hugged and kissed and lay on the carpet holding hands and giggling. It was the greatest day of our lives. 'A feast!' I said jumping up. 'Invitations must be sent, cooks engaged, new uniforms made for the maids, there is spring cleaning to be done! We will call it the Feast of Cleopatra's Cat!' The girls both clapped and laughed at this grand notion, after all it was Cleopatra's Cat who had saved us from despair and kept our hopes alive.

You can imagine our excitement when the train pulled in. We wanted to look wonderful for Uri's arrival, his three pretty women.

I had bought a new outfit for each of us. Tanya and Anna both wore pale blue taffeta dresses with grown-up mutton leg sleeves, matching blue ribbons in their hair, and the new, single-strap English style button-across patent leather shoes. I wore a chocolate-brown grosgrain costume that fitted tightly round the waist with a flare at the top of the hips, and a tapered skirt that boldly showed a snatch of ankle above red shoes with an outrageously high six-centimetre heel, the latest in Parisian fashion. All of this was set off by a beautiful hat decorated with scarlet and blue French ribbon and a peacock feather that seemed to brush the summer sky.

We looked frantically for Uri among the bustling crowd, not quite knowing what to expect. Would he be thin as a rake, aged, with his hair prematurely white? Would he be dressed in rags? Or using a walking stick? We didn't know what to expect. But I didn't care what he looked like, I simply wanted his big surgeon's hands to be wrapped around me, our little family all together again.

But eventually the platform was empty, even the porters had taken their barrows piled high with baggage, and only the two girls and myself were left standing on the platform. The engine hissed intermittently, its *sshhh* of steam somehow adding to the silence and the desolation of the empty station. Then an official in a smart uniform and cap stepped off the train and walked purposefully towards us.

'Mrs Shebaldin?'

I nodded.

'Follow me, please.' Without any further explanation he turned and walked towards the end of the train.

Of course! I suddenly thought. Uri is ill, why didn't I think of that! Relief flooded through me.

'What is it, Mama?' Tanya asked, sensing my anxiety and then my sudden relief. Anna grabbed my hand, saying nothing, a little girl again.

'I don't know, darling,' I replied. 'Perhaps your papa is not well.'

We stopped at the very end carriage. It was different from the other carriages, with no windows, only ventilation slits high up on blank sides. The official produced a set of keys and unlocked the carriage door. It was a heavy door and he had to force it open with his shoulder.

'He is in there, madam.' He pointed at the dark interior of the carriage and then turned and looked down the platform. 'Have you not made arrangements to have him removed?' Then he shrugged and pushed the clipboard under my nose. 'Sign here, please. There are two items, a sealed lead coffin and one live cat in a large birdcage.'

Slow tears run down Sophia Shebaldin's face and I see that Anya and Tamara are both weeping softly and that Mr Mendelsohn is also sniffing. I must admit a big lump is also sitting in my throat and I can barely see the Family Frying Pan bubbling away on the fire.

'There was a letter in a false bottom of Cleopatra's Cat's cage,' Sophia says slowly. 'A wonderful long letter, it was from a fellow prisoner and I have it here with me.'

She reaches into the bodice of her dress and brings out a

small linen bag. Her long, hard fingers work at the knot which ties the end and Sophia Shebaldin removes the letter. There is a full moon and it is quite light enough to read and now she looks up, the light from the moon softening her small, sharp features. Then she begins to read.

Dear Madam Shebaldin,

I am writing to you as a friend and great admirer of the late and truly great surgeon, Uri Shebaldin. Or should I say, Sir Uri Shebaldin, Surgeon to the Queen of Egypt? Uri died this morning in the company of five thousand men who loved him and will mourn him every day that remains of their short and precarious lives.

Allow me to explain, madam. Life in a Gulag is measured by the extent to which a man will struggle to survive, whether at the expense of another is of no importance. Feeling and compassion are luxuries reserved for those who are free; here survival is the only purpose and measure of a man's worth. A man who would think otherwise would not last a month in this place. That is, any other man but your husband.

I was in the cattle truck with him when he first produced the tiny ginger kitten from his pocket and held it up. There was, I recall, a great deal of laughter at the tiny creature held aloft and one of the prisoners shouted, 'It is not even sufficient for a poor man's breakfast!' Uri laughed along with all of us, but then he said, 'If it survives, comrades, then we all survive! This cat will be our talisman! A cat has nine lives and we are going to need every one of them if we are ever to return from Siberia to our loved ones.'

Men are superstitious creatures and from that moment the little ginger kitten became very important to us all. Somehow we kept it alive on the long journey to Siberia and when we arrived at the Gulag we took turns to protect the kitten from becoming a tasty morsel for a starving prisoner who was not in our group.

Here in the slave camps unremitting hunger is our constant companion. A small slice of black bread and a dish of hot water, with perhaps a rotten slice of carrot and a lump of potato no bigger than your thumb, are all we get from the authorities; the rest we must find for ourselves. We all carry small forage tins on our belts and as we work we look for things to eat, a few fat grubs under a piece of bark or some small plant root, or edible leaf. Sometimes, if we are lucky, a wild mushroom, though very little grows in the tundra. When it rains things are better, this is the time when the earthworms come to the surface and a man can gather a dozen or more in his tin if he is lucky. They are very good to eat. (To a starving man, any protein is a gift from God!)

But, no matter how hungry we were, if our cat passed by, any of us would give her a share of our worms. Cleopatra's Cat was not only loved but also very useful. In the dry weather she could locate earthworms under the soil and many a man was saved from starvation by her remarkable nose for this hidden protein. When she killed a rat we would give her the head and the tail and the rest would go into the pot. Any prisoner attempting to turn the cat into a meal would have been instantly killed. Cleopatra's Cat became the sign to us that survival in the salt mines was possible and that we would someday go home again.

But it was not only the cat that kept our hopes up, it was also the letters the cat wrote and your replies. They were smuggled in from the hospital and passed from hand to hand and read aloud to those who could not read. Your little family became at once all our families and we took to thinking of ourselves as 'the Egyptians'. You gave us something to hope for.

You see, madam, Uri Shebaldin was everything Cleopatra's Cat said he was in her letters from Egypt. He was a diplomat with the authorities, often saving a prisoner from a terrible beating or even death at the hand of a guard or camp official. Moreover, his scalpel worked ceaselessly in the little cottage hospital.

For instance, on the very first night we arrived he saved the life of the son of the camp commandant by removing a brain tumour. In the past five years his remarkable hands have saved hundreds of lives.

I am a doctor myself, though only a humble pill-pusher. For the sake of Uri's colleagues at the Academy of Medicine in St Petersburg I shall enumerate some of these medical breakthroughs. His post-operative notes are included with this letter for the benefit of students and teachers at the academy.

Uri Shebaldin has developed techniques for removing gastric and duodenal ulcers and has performed what he terms gastroectomies (notes attached). He has, with a high degree of success, removed cancers from the large bowel and the rectum and developed a method whereby he operates on cancer of the rectum through the area between the anus and the genitals.

You must excuse my language, Madam Shebaldin, but you are a medical family and I know will take no exception to this terminology. Finally, Uri Shebaldin has become the absolute master of the appendectomy, saving countless lives with this one operative procedure alone.

Uri died after a typhoid epidemic in the slave camps where he worked incessantly to save others' lives. His dying wish was that we should try to return Cleopatra's Cat to little

Anna and Tanya and that you should know the hope you have brought to thousands of condemned men. But for your letters they would have died long before completing their sentences. Despair is the true epidemic of Siberia. Now many believe they will return to their homes and some already have. Uri did not write because he believed he would not return and he hoped his dear family would eventually forget him and live normal lives again.

I must confess that several of the men asked that you not be told of your husband's death as they have become addicted to the letters from Egypt. But decency and a love of Surgeon Shebaldin prevailed, not an ordinary occurrence in a place where both these commodities are almost unknown. Your husband asked that, if Cleopatra's Cat should come home, you hold a great feast for her and, at the same time, light a candle in his memory. He also fervently desires that you should marry again and be \ happy.

We have persuaded the authorities to return his body to you, though it is sealed in lead and may not be opened for fear that the typhoid may spread. You must honour your husband by complying strictly with this request. Besides, he would wish you to remember him as he was when he left his beloved family.

My own sentence has five years yet to run and I do not

suppose I shall leave this place alive. May God bless you and your children. It remains only for me to say that my life has been made richer by the gifts of your husband – whom I counted as my friend and colleague – your letters from Egypt and, of course, Cleopatra's Cat. I hope she will survive a difficult journey accompanying the body of Sir Uri Shebaldin, Surgeon to the Queen of Egypt.

My salutations to your two lovely daughters. I remain, madam, your faithful admirer,

Alexander Proknikoff – Medical Doctor.

Sophia Shebaldin completes her reading, sad as the contents are; we are all filled with admiration for her.

Now she continues: 'What a feast was prepared, and Cleopatra's Cat was the centre of attention as students and teachers from the Academy of Medicine and all our friends celebrated Uri's death in true Russian style. His notes were welcomed at the academy and he was hailed as a true hero of Mother Russia. A year later the Tsar presented me with the Medal of Honour, Second Class, and a military band played at the ceremony in the great square outside the Winter Palace. At the presentation the principal of the academy spoke of Uri as a remarkable surgeon and announced that a new and modern operating theatre would be built in his honour and named after him.'

Sophia Shebaldin looks up and gives a brief smile. 'My

beloved husband had been completely exonerated and now Mother Russia clasped our little family to her fond bosom. The so-called Bolshevik surgeon was the hero of the hour and those who had brought about his downfall now hurried to kiss my hand.'

Sophia Shebaldin pauses and looks around. 'I thank you for your patience and for taking me into your small group. I feel humble that you would welcome me.' She smiled, looking at each of us in turn. 'And that, my dear friends is the end of my little story.'

We all clap furiously, it is a wonderful tale. Of course, the one question on all of our minds is how, with all the honours and posthumous fame bestowed on Uri Shebaldin, she should come to be in our little group, which is definitely no place for the rich and famous. But I am glad to say we all hold our tongues, even Olga Zorbatov remains *stum*.

Tonight we eat with relish. After all, it is not every night we are privileged to hear a good story and, at the same time, enjoy a truly delicious horsemeat stew.

When we have finished eating, to our surprise and, I must say, delight, Sophia Shebaldin offers to tell us the remainder of her remarkable adventure.

'I wanted that you should eat in a happy frame of mind,' she explains. It was a lovely dinner tonight, Mrs Moses, and I didn't want to spoil it with talk of sorrow.' She pauses. 'I thank you for your good manners, for not demanding to know how I have come to be with all of you on the road to freedom.'

We all grin rather sheepishly.

'The great influenza epidemic of 1907 took Tanya and little Anna,' Sophia Shebaldin says quietly and then she begins to weep. I go to put my arm around her, but she gently pushes me away. 'I am such a coward,' she sobs, 'but I could bear it no longer. Mother Russia has destroyed us completely, there is no more happiness for me in this cruel land.'

She sniffs and lifts her chin defiantly. 'I shall go to London where I will search for a ginger cat. Then, together, we will take the boat to Egypt where I will sit on the edge of the desert and dream and my English cat will nap in the sun. I shall put up a sign outside my little home which reads '"Foot Doctor". There will always be people who suffer from sore and weary feet. I shall restore them and send them on their way. An old woman and a ginger cat, whom I shall name Sir Frederick Treves, do not require much to stay alive.' She looks up and although the night is warm she appears to shiver. 'My bones are so very cold, I go to warm them in the desert sunlight and to rest at night under an Arabian sky pricked by a million stars.'

There is silence and then, to my surprise, Mr Petrov speaks. 'And what happened to Cleopatra's Cat, Madam Shebaldin?'

Sophia Shebaldin laughs, a genuine laugh that comes from her belly, one we have never heard before. It is pretty and lighthearted and makes us all feel good. Then she spreads her arms wide and shrugs. 'You know cats,' Mr Petrov. They don't like to be moved. Cleopatra's Cat was last seen catching the train back to Siberia. If you ask me, another *cat*-astrophe in the making!'

Cleopatra's CAKE

²/₃ cup/170 g/6 oz **butter**, softened

1 cup/220 g/7³/₄ oz **castor sugar**

grated zest of 2 lemons

1 teaspoon **vanilla essence**

²/₃ cup **fresh poppyseeds**

2 cups/280 g/10 oz **self-raising flour**, sifted

1 cup/250 ml/8 fl oz **milk**

4 **egg whites**

ICING

¹/₂ cup/120 g/4 oz **butter or margarine**, softened

1¹/₃ cups/180 g/6 oz **icing sugar**, sifted

a few drops **vanilla essence**

4 drops **red food colouring**

METHOD

Preheat the oven to 180°C/350°F/gas mark 4.

Butter and line the base of a 22 cm/9 in springform tin with baking paper.

In a large mixing bowl, cream the butter until soft, then gradually add the sugar, taking care to beat well between each addition. Add the zest, vanilla essence and poppyseeds.

Fold through some of the flour, then the milk, alternately until well combined.

Whisk the egg whites in a separate bowl until stiff peaks form. Fold the whites quickly and lightly through the poppyseed mixture, and spoon into the prepared tin.

Bake in the preheated oven for about 1 hour or until a skewer inserted through the middle comes out clean.

Allow to cool in the tin for 15 minutes, then turn out onto a cake rack to cool completely before icing.

To make the icing, cream the butter until smooth. Add the icing sugar and cream until smooth. Add the vanilla essence and food colouring until the desired colour is achieved.

Makes 1 × 22 cm/9 in cake

To the Four Winds

THESE ARE SOME OF THE STORIES THAT MY

great-grandmother told her family, long before I was born, of course. They all went into my grandfather's tape recorder. I have tried to tell the stories exactly as she did on Friday nights during *Shabbat*, after they'd lit the candles and blessed the wine.

If you've read the stories you'll see that every once in a while I mention the presence of children. But you haven't been told the story of the children. I suppose this was because kids don't sit around and tell their own stories until they're grown up.

As many children as adults accompanied Mrs Moses on her journey out of the wilderness and they became much loved by all. Now comes the big surprise! When it came time to split up, with each person following their own dream, it was Olga Zorbatov who insisted on taking all the children.

'They are a family,' she insisted, 'they should not be parted from each other.'

The children in the group belonged to no one, but of course they were free to go their own way if they wished. They had simply joined the journey along the way and were nobody's children. Left alone they would have almost certainly come to a sad ending, most likely they'd have grown up to be thieves, drunkards and prostitutes. That is, if they didn't die of starvation or some disease. In those days just having the flu could kill a person.

Strays and orphans that they were, for the children the great trek out of Russia under the leadership and the love of Mrs Moses was the first time had ever experienced affection. Although Olga Zorbatov could be a real pain in the you-know-what to all of the adults, the kids loved her even more than they loved Anya, which is saying quite a lot.

The Mrs Moses group eventually crossed into Poland where the Polish authorities, sick and tired of people fleeing out of Russia, put them into a cattle truck and moved them to the German border.

Mrs Moses and her little group were most grateful for the lift across Poland, a country they collectively regarded as being very little improvement on Russia. In Germany they noticed that a lot of marching was going on and that there seemed to be sol-diers everywhere. Mrs Moses had had enough of soldiers, whom she saw as the same old hunters, whatever their uniform.

She appealed to a Jewish refugee agency which provided them with train tickets and food to get them to Paris. It was only when they arrived in Paris that they finally broke up and went their separate ways.

I'm sure there must have been many tears and hugs and promises made to stay in touch, though my great-grandmother either didn't comment on this sad moment or my grandfather lost the tape with that bit on. Anyway, they scattered to the four winds. But, it seems, they never entirely escaped the long arm of Mrs Moses, because she has recorded all their subsequent stories.

The Twelve Lost Tribes of California

Olga Zorbatov and her twelve children eventually got to California and then to the city of Los Angeles. Her husband Sergei was still sending her nightly messages from the stars and so she set up as a psychic.

Her timing was perfect. Nestled among the orange groves in the tiny hamlet of Hollywood was the fledgling movie industry. The silent movies needed kids and Olga Zorbatov had twelve hungry mouths to feed. Her dozen little ragamuffins who worked as a team were a movie director's dream. They could and would do anything for a laugh and seemed to have no fear. Maybe you've seen some of those very old silent movies on TV?

For instance, the kids in Mack Sennett's first Hollywood movies were mostly Mrs Z's orphans.

Mrs Z had given all the children the same surname, though not her own. When she had landed at Ellis Island in New York the clerk had sighed. 'These are your children, Mrs Zorbatov? Give me their names, please.'

'Moses, all are Moses!' Mrs Z declared.

The immigration officer was accustomed to confusion and he sighed heavily again. It was going to be a long day. 'All are called Moses Zorbatov, even the girls?'

Olga Zorbatov was losing patience. 'No, me I am Zorbatov, they Moses!' She grabbed a small girl. 'Tanya Moses!' Then she pointed to a boy. 'Ivan Moses!'

The official nodded. 'And where is Mrs Moses?' he asked.

'She go to Australia,' Olga declared.

'With twelve children who can blame her?' the weary immigration officer said, then began the task of writing down the Christian names of the children and appending Moses to each of them.

Olga Zorbatov, in honour of Mrs Moses having led them out of the wilderness, had given all the children her surname. Because there were twelve children she likened it to Moses leading the twelve tribes of Israel out of bondage. She was not a Jew herself, nor, for that matter, were any of the children, but for one small boy named Moshe. She told them that each of them came from one of the eleven lost tribes of Israel, while

Moshe with the missing foreskin was kosher; that is to say, he came from the Hebrew tribe, the one that didn't manage to get itself lost.

With her fortune-telling and her children playing crowd scenes and bit parts and running messages on the film lots, Olga was able to survive, and it was her boast that her lost tribes had found the promised land and had never gone without a meal in America.

Then, one day, she hit upon her one really big idea. She decided to open the first casting agency in Hollywood.

Actually, it wasn't her idea, and in truth she never claimed it was, giving all the credit instead to her husband from whom she still now claimed to take nightly instructions as he schlepped across the midnight sky, riding on the tail of this or that sign of the zodiac. She named her agency Casting to the Stars, not because the word 'star' had any meaning in the movie industry at that time, but because her beloved husband (she seemed to have completely forgotten that she had murdered him) instructed that she should name it after the star-studded firmament.

In fact, so successful was Mrs Z at picking acting talent that the very word 'star' as a description for actors who made the big time is derived from the name of her casting agency. The agency survives to this day, though under a different name. Apparently she had neglected to register the name and so the phrase Casting to the Stars was pinched by other casting consultancies which emerged over the years and became a cliché.

When this happened Mrs Z changed the name of her agency to Central Casting of Hollywood.

Olga Zorbatov never married ('Sergei would kill me!') and she eventually died in 1955 at the age of eighty. Her funeral was attended by ten of her lost tribes, including Moshe, who, by that time, was running a big Hollywood studio. They came to pay their respects, together with thirty-nine of her grandchildren and one hundred and three great-grandchildren.

In her last will and testament she left nearly eight million dollars to establish a Chair of Astrological Science at the University of California. It is no coincidence that the State of California has been producing highly intelligent nutcases and weirdos ever since.

The Chickens Who Loved Tchaikovsky

Of Anya and Mr Mendelsohn a quieter story. They too went to America, straight to Boston, where Mr Mendelsohn was disappointed to find that the famous symphony orchestra was not for sale, not even for all the pearls in the South Sea.

However, he did eventually become the orchestra's First Violin. He married Anya in the Russian Orthodox Church in Boston, which was what she wanted. In return Anna gave him two more sons and made him chicken and mushroom soup every night of his life.

Alas, the soup was not as good as her Russian concoctions had been, and Anna often lamented that she was unable to find the various types of mushrooms she required. She also complained about the chickens. 'American chickens eat the wrong kind of worms,' she'd say. 'Maybe making a living for worms is too easy in America and they don't work hard enough to give the chicken meat the best flavour. Also, there is no blue corn to feed them.' And then later in her life, when battery hens came into vogue, she got really angry and cashed in the last of the mermaid's pearls and started her own chicken farm.

When Mr Mendelsohn eventually retired from the Boston Symphony Orchestra he would play to the chickens morning and night. 'It's not maybe so glamorous as mermaids,' he would say, 'but, believe me, a chicken has better taste in music.' In fact, Anya's chickens loved his whole repertoire and in particular Tchaikovsky. This especially endeared them to him and they returned the compliment by laying the best eggs in America. Anya imported worms and mushroom spawn from Russia and a sack of best blue corn which she sowed by hand in the traditional peasant manner. The worms thrived in her compost heap, the mushrooms flourished in the dark of a disused horse stable, and the corn took to the more democratic American climate which resulted in one bumper crop after another. Soon Mr Mendelsohn was enjoying chicken soup second to none, the best in the world, whatever country you care to name in chicken soup competition, including Israel.

Their three sons grew to manhood and together they opened a restaurant called Mr Mendelsohn's Chicken Spit, which sold barbecued chicken and chicken and mushroom soup (six varieties of mushroom skilfully blended). Later, as they expanded, they adapted the name of their several restaurants to Mr Chicken Spit, a chain which boasted that it used only free-range chickens and White Russian field mushrooms (the Cold War was still on). Today, with the feminist movement in full swing, it is called The Chicken Spit and is a franchise operation which has eight hundred outlets in America and another six hundred throughout the world. Next year the first Chicken Spit in Russia opens in Red Square, directly opposite Lenin's tomb. Anya's grandchild, Michael Mendelsohn, who graduated *summa cum laude* at MIT with a Master of Science in Food Technology, is now chief executive of CSI Inc. – Chicken Spit International – and will be there with the Senator for Massachusetts, who will officially open the first Eastern European franchise.

It's a great pity that Anya and Mr Mendelsohn never lived to see this triumphant return to Mother Russia, though, admittedly he would have been one hundred and eleven years old and she one hundred and sixteen.

Mr Mendelsohn died of a heart attack in 1961 while listening to Tchaikovsky's Symphony No. 4 on the radio. When Anya found him in his old leather armchair he still had a smile on his face.

That night Anya made chicken and mushroom soup and then sat quietly beside Mr Mendelsohn, whom she had bathed and dressed in his best silk pyjamas and put into the bed they had shared for nearly fifty years. She sat beside him with the steaming bowl on a tray on her lap. 'I loved you, Mr Mermaid Man,' she said quietly, 'every day of our wonderful life.' The next morning a neighbour found her dead, still seated beside her beloved violinist, his beautiful hands with the long, elegant fingers clasped in her own.

At the autopsy, traces of *Entoloma sinuatum* were found in Anya's stomach. It is also known as the Poison Chalice and is another of the clever little mushrooms a peasant girl from a Russian village makes it her business to know all about in case someday it comes in useful.

A Hero of Leningrad

And now news of Tamara Polyansky, who also went to America and became one of the leading attractions of the great Barnum & Bailey Circus.

But not all stories turn out happily ever after, and while Tamara enjoyed great notoriety and top billing in the famous circus, she was never really happy in America. She found it difficult to understand the American people who appeared so friendly, inviting you into their homes after a five-minute acquaintance, but who seemed reluctant to enter into any deeper relationship. 'America,' she would say, 'is a mile wide and an inch deep; Russia is an inch wide and a mile deep. That is why we will never understand each other.'

Tamara Polyansky seemed to have everything – fame, fortune and beauty. But what she craved more than anything was love. While she despaired of ever finding another great love like Eugene Wilenski, love has more than one face and she hoped to find a partner who would hold her in his adoring arms while they made wonderful love. Tamara was a romantic dreamer in the land where romance is bought with hard currency.

What is perhaps strangest of all, Tamara longed for Siberia where she had spent the first years of her circus life. Life in the circus was frantic and often quarrelsome, full of petty jealousy and back stabbing, each performer competing with the other for a higher billing on the circus posters or a bigger name in lights on the Big Top. Moreover, circuses in America were often attached to country fairs, rodeos, Fourth of July parades and all the razzamatazz of an immature people, and Tamara, increasingly, longed for the quiet of the endless tundra and the deep respect Russians hold for a great artist.

My great-grandma always claimed that Tamara's desire for solitude was probably some sort of romantic notion brought about by too much suffering and tragedy in her life. She pointed out that the Russian personality is very big on suffering and the American not at all keen on it, so Tamara may have come to believe that what she now craved was the solitude of Siberia, having entirely forgotten how awful it had been in the first place.

Tamara tried to leave the circus when she met and married a dashing American flier from Nebraska, five years younger than herself. Not a trapeze flier, but an airman who flew a Sopwith Camel in the United States Air Corps. But tragedy struck once more when her young husband was shot down and killed over France on the first day the Americans saw combat in the air during the Great War, in 1917.

He was shot down by an Australian infantry soldier who, not recognising the insignia painted on the wings of the by-plane, thought it must belong to the enemy. By some incredible fluke he hit Tamara's airman between the eyes with a single bullet from his Lee Enfield rifle. He got reprimanded and Tamara got the usual 'Killed in Action' telegram from Washington.

'Must all the men in my life be shot out of the sky!' was all she said. Then, dry-eyed, she packed her bags.

With the death of her American airman and with the advent of the Russian Revolution that same year, Tamara remembered the parting words of Count Tolstoy as he lay dying in the little railway station shed. 'Child, leave Russia and return only when the Tsar and those like him have been overthrown.' Miss Showbiz decided to take the advice of the world's greatest writer and she returned to Moscow.

For many years after her return she and Mrs Moses exchanged

letters and it seemed that Tamara was happy enough. The communists, anxious to stamp their mark on the proletariat, made her a professor at the Academy of Circus and Ballet in Moscow where she taught acrobatics, the high wire and trapeze, and so became a founding member of the now world-famous Moscow Circus. For her brilliant work she was made a Hero of the Soviet Union and, surprisingly, just before the Second World War she was also made a colonel in the military forces and posted to a circus training school in Leningrad to help train an entertainment battalion for the Red Army.

The last letter Mrs Moses received from Tamara Polyansky was in April 1941, and the Germans invaded the USSR in June that same year. It took Hitler only two and a half months to reach the outskirts of Leningrad, which, as the birthplace of Bolshevism, he swore to wipe from the face of the earth.

German troops began the siege of Leningrad on the 8th of September 1941, and continued until the 27th of January 1944. In Russian history, this great siege where ordinary people resisted the might of the greatest invasion in Russian history, is simply called Nine Hundred Days.

By the time the Germans withdrew from Leningrad, defeated and utterly demoralised, a million Russian civilians and foot soldiers had perished defending the city. Many died from the ceaseless shelling, but as many more dropped dead of hunger and cold in the streets. And when no dogs, cats or rats were left to eat they ate the glue off the back of wallpaper. Mrs Moses prayed to God for every one of those nine hundred days and begged that He should spare Miss Showbiz.

In 1950 my great-grandmother received a letter and a small package from the Russian Department of War Veterans to say that Colonel Tamara Polyansky had died in the Siege of Leningrad defending her country. They had found her last will and testament which had been lodged before her posting to Leningrad, as was required by the Department of the Soviet Army in Moscow. She had left all her worldly possessions to Mrs Moses, 107 Campbell Parade, Bondi Beach, Sydney, Australia. The letter went on to say that Colonel Polyansky's body had never been found and that there were no worldly possessions to inherit, but that to honour her name the USSR enclosed for Mrs Moses the Medal of Hero of the Soviet Union, an inheritance more valuable to a Russian than life itself.

Poor Miss Showbiz, I hope she had some happy years jammed in somewhere between all the tragedy in her life. Of all the people Mrs Moses led out of the wilderness I think I liked her the best. When my great-grandmother died in 1965 she was buried with the medal awarded to Colonel Tamara Polyansky pinned to her chest. She said she would personally return it to its rightful owner when she got to Heaven.

1 cup/250 ml/8 fl oz
chicken stock

1 medium white onion,
finely chopped

1 large bunch spinach,
stalks removed and finely
chopped

150 g/5 oz fetta cheese,
crumbled

½ teaspoon nutmeg,
freshly grated

½ teaspoon cinnamon

1 tablespoon fresh dill,
finely chopped

black pepper, freshly
ground

¼ cup pine nuts, toasted

9 sheets filo pastry,
halved lengthwise

¼ cup/60 g/2 oz butter,
melted

lemon wedges

Siberian SPINACH Sensation

METHOD

Bring the chicken stock to the boil in a large saucepan. Add the chopped onion. Reduce the heat, cover and simmer for 5 minutes.

Add the spinach, cover and simmer until tender, about 3 to 4 minutes. Remove the spinach and onion from the pan and drain off the excess liquid.

Add the fetta cheese, nutmeg, cinnamon, dill, pepper and pine nuts to the spinach mixture. Mix well to combine and allow to cool to room temperature.

Preheat the oven to 180°C/350°F/gas mark 4. Lightly grease a baking tray.

Brush each sheet of filo with melted butter. Take a small amount of the spinach mixture and place on the lower edge of the pastry sheet. Make a roll, tuck in the edges, and continue rolling. Make up the rest of the rolls in this way. Brush the rolls with melted butter and place on the baking tray. Bake for 45 minutes until golden brown, and serve immediately with lemon wedges.

Makes 18

The Professor and Whacker's Sulphur-crested Cockatoo

The professor's story is a bit different from the rest of Mrs Moses' little flock. He elected to go to England and when he was asked why he would choose it over America, or one of the newer countries like Australia or New Zealand or even South Africa, he shrugged. 'We have Shakespeare in common with the English, that is not a bad start.'

'Shakespeare? What has Russia got to do with Shakespeare? Tolstoy, who is practically still living, yes, but that Englishman is long dead and probably he never even came to Russia,' Mrs Moses exclaimed when he announced his intention.

'Russian is the only language other than English in which the works of Shakespeare translate perfectly,' the professor said. 'Our minds beat to the same rhythm, our tongues to the same cadence, and that is enough for me. I shall go to England, the English are the only truly civilised Russians!'

And that was that. Sometimes after hearing the professor carrying on Mrs Moses took the trouble to thank the Lord that she wasn't clever.

However, it seems the professor must have known something because before you could say 'Stratford upon Avon' he had been granted a fellowship at Oxford University in the Department of Russian Literature. And, it seems, he soon became famous, not so much for his lectures on Tolstoy, Dostoyevsky and Pushkin but for his bird-watching.

The English are notorious bird-watchers, or 'twitchers' as they are commonly called, and it seems that English academics and intellectuals are particularly keen on putting on wellies and wading into marshes, getting cold, wet, hungry and devoured by insects, or climbing into trees or hides until their bones ache with fatigue, simply to see the first robin in spring or the departure of the last swallow in autumn. The professor was soon upgraded to professorial status again, not because his insights into the works of Aleksandr Sergeyevich Pushkin or Fyodor Mikhailovich Dostoyevsky were all that remarkable, but because he seemed to know more about birds than anyone else at the world-famous university. Knowledge of such high order could not be invested in a lowly don and so he was immediately elevated to the rank of professor.

Under the patronage of the collective twitchers of England, who bought his books on exotic species of birds by the tens of thousands and attended his lectures to the Gould and Audobon Societies, the professor grew even more puffed up and pompous and soon he was as stuffy and incomprehensible as all the other academics at Oxford. At which stage the English decided he was as close to being an Englishman as he was ever going to get, and that it was time to grant him full citizenship. He accepted in the name of Russia and of Shakespeare.

'The English are really Russians in disguise!' he was fond of saying. 'Shakespeare would have made an excellent Russian.'

The professor also corresponded with Mrs Moses in Australia. His letters tended to be long and complex and, for the most part, contained questions about parrots, galahs, budgerigars and cockatoos. Mrs Moses would take his letters down to the Bondi Pet Shop and asked the owner, Whacker O'Sullivan, for the information the professor required. Whacker would scratch his head. 'Never thought a flamin' budgie needed to be that complicated, Mrs Mo, but seeing as I'm the expert I'll let you have the info by termorra, orright?'

He knew a bloke at the Australian Museum who drank at the same pub as him. The man from the museum usually knew the answers to just about everything and Whacker didn't want Mrs

Moses to know he knew sweet Fanny Adams about budgies. It was no use simply talking to the expert, Whacker couldn't remember his own name after a few beers, so he made the man from the museum write the information on a cigarette paper.

When Mrs Moses came into the shop the next day he pretended to make a roll-yer-own and, in a normal, casual sort of voice which disguised the fact that he was reading from the cigarette paper, told her what the bloke from the museum had written down. This little information scam continued every time Mrs Moses received a letter from the professor.

After a few years, with Mrs Moses telling everyone about his expertise and with the professor himself mentioning his name as an authority on the parrots of the Antipodes in one of his famous bird books sent to Mrs Moses, Whacker O'Sullivan was considered to be a leading Australian expert on the genus.

That is, until the expert from the museum died of cirrhosis of the liver and Whacker was forced into having amnesia, brought about, he insisted, by a punch in the head sustained in a pub brawl. 'Me bird brain's gorn, Mrs Mo, can't remember a flamin' thing about them cockies no more.'

But at about the time Whacker O'Sullivan's bird brain was irrevocably destroyed, the professor's letters began to change. The Bolsheviks had taken over Russia in the 1917 revolution and the Tsar and his family were murdered by the Reds, although their bodies were never discovered.

The effect on the professor was profound. He had loved the Princess Tatiana like his own daughter and he took the news of her death very badly. He seemed to lose all interest in life and his morbid letters dwelt on the reported death of the princess and precluded any mention of parrots, cockatoos, parakeets, galahs or budgerigars.

After a while the professor's letters took what seemed, at first, a turn for the better. He'd convinced himself that, because the bodies of the Russian royal family had never been found, the Reds hadn't killed them. His theory was that they had been allowed to escape under one condition – that they never revealed their true identities to the outside world.

Mrs Moses hoped that the professor would let it rest at that and resume his interest in birds. But another letter soon followed which told her that the professor had decided to dedicate the rest of his life to flushing out the Russian royals.

Mrs Moses, reading between the lines, realised that the professor, who had always been a bit, you know, funny, had finally gone over the top, or, to use her own expression, was now plain *meshuggana*. So when Whacker O'Sullivan, who had gotten used to feeling important, asked why the professor hadn't written in quite a while, Mrs Moses confided that she was worried about her dear friend.

Mrs Moses tearfully told Whacker how the professor had become obsessed with the notion that the Tsar and his family had escaped and were living incognito somewhere out of Russia.

'Yeah?' Whacker said. 'Where you suppose they gorn, Mrs Mo?'

Mrs Moses hastened to point out to Whacker in her somewhat broken English that this was a highly unlikely theory, as you couldn't go around hiding an entire Russian royal family without someone eventually cottoning on.

Whacker thought about this for a while and then, naturally, he took the problem down to the pub with him. The way he told the story to the blokes there, the Russian royal family had escaped the Reds but were all suffering from amnesia and were last seen boarding the boat in Southhampton bound for Australia.

'Crikey, we could have flamin' royalty walking along Bondi Beach not knowing who the blazes they are!' was how he ended his sad tale.

While most of the drinkers thought this an unlikely story there were some who, while not being exactly intellectually challenged, were definitely on the naïve side and after a few more beers the rumour that the Russian royal family had been seen on Bondi Beach was taken home by every drunk with an Irish name in the pub, which meant practically everyone present after eight o'clock that night.

By morning Bondi Beach was awash with the rumour and by noon everyone was looking hard at anyone they didn't recognise as a local to see if he or she looked as though they might be a Russian. Not that anyone knew what a Russian was supposed to look like. 'Sort of foreign looking with heavy eyebrows and women with long plaits and dark eyes who wear embroidered peasant blouses but who you can see aren't, you know, your proper wogs. Oh yes, and the men wearing high boots with the top of their pants tucked in.'

Fortunately it was winter and there were only a few people on the beach. But by four o'clock that afternoon an Italian with dark and heavy eyebrows from Leichhardt, an inner-city suburb, had been spotted paddling on the beach with his wife and five children. There was also a pair of suspicious looking knee-high boots on the sand nearby and the man had his pants rolled up to his knees. This was evidence enough and the Russian royal family was promptly rounded up by a big crowd of locals who escorted the loudly protesting husband and wife and their five tearful children to the police station.

Whacker O'Sullivan, stepping from the crowd, announced to Sergeant Bumper O'Flynn that the Ruski royals had been found wandering aimlessly along the beach, and that it was obvious they were suffering from amnesia and it was his civic duty to turn them in to the authorities.

When Bumper O'Flynn looked a trifle doubtful, Whacker duly pointed out that he was an expert in memory loss and so should recognise the condition when he came across it. 'Besides, can't you hear them, they're bloody yacking away in Russian, aren't they, mate?'

'Sounds more like I-talian to me,' the police sergeant suggested.

'Nah! It's fair-dinkum Russian orright,' Whacker insisted.

As the Italian and his wife had not long arrived in Australia and couldn't yet speak English they were yabbering away in a Sicilian dialect, which naturally enough everyone now took to be Russian. As nobody could understand Russian, Mrs Moses was immediately sent for.

In her traditional no-nonsense manner she soon got things sorted out and afterwards she got really cranky with Whacker O'Sullivan for creating such a ridiculous incident. Whacker, at heart a gentleman, was truly contrite and in an effort to mollify Mrs Moses he offered to give the professor a sulphur-crested cockatoo, which would be delivered by a mate of his who was the second engineer on the *Duke of York*, a passenger steamer that sailed regularly between England and Australia.

Mrs Moses was much taken by this idea. With such a handsome bird as his companion, the professor might snap out of his preoccupation with the whereabouts of the Tsar and his family. The cocky was duly delivered by Whacker's engineer mate and a happy ending was hoped for by all.

But it was not to be. The professor's obsession grew worse. He had convinced himself that the Russian royal family had escaped and were living as poor relations with their second cousin King George in Buckingham Palace. Furthermore, he wrote, they were being kept in captivity against their will.

Before he went completely crazy the professor wrote to Mrs Moses to say that the lovely white cockatoo with the brilliant

yellow plumage was a most excellent friend and that it personally and continually strengthened his resolve to find the missing
Russian royals and to expose the King of England. This was
probably because Whacker, who was still far from convinced
that the professor's theory was incorrect, hadn't told Mrs Moses
that he'd taught the cocky to say, 'The princess lives! The
princess lives!'

The ending is maybe sad and maybe not, it all depends on
how you look at life. The professor, by now supposedly impov-
erished, spent the remainder of his days outside Buckingham
Palace with a sandwich board draped over his ancient greatcoat. Painted on the board were the words: 'Free Russian royal
family – the Tsar is a bird-watcher!'

Never separated from the professor was the beautiful
Australian sulphur-crested cockatoo, who sat on his shoulder
squawking, 'The princess lives! The princess lives!' What's more,
every day, winter and summer, all the birds of the air, the robins,
wrens, thrushes, cockfinches, larks, sparrows and the rest, would
come and visit, pecking at the breadcrumbs the professor would
habitually rub into his snowy beard. People would stop and
watch in wonder and most would leave a coin or two in the battered trilby hat which lay at the professor's feet. In fact, so popular a tourist attraction did the old man become that the hat filled
with coins several times a day and the professor was forced to
take a taxi to Barclays Bank in Knightsbridge every evening and
then home to where he lived under Chelsea Bridge.

When Professor Ivan Mikhaylovich Slotinowitz died in 1938 he received a splendid obituary in *The Times* of London. The obituary mentioned in passing that he had left a bequest of ten thousand pounds to go towards building an aviary at London Zoo.

What with the Second World War and everything, the bequest was sort of forgotten and it was more than twenty years later, with the interest on the original capital having accumulated, that the great aviary was commissioned by the custodians of London Zoo to be designed by Lord Snowdon. The professor would have liked this a lot, Lord Snowdon having once been married to Princess Margaret who is a distant cousin to Princess Tatiana.

Oh yes, I almost forgot, the only condition attached to the bequest was that the aviary should contain, at the very least, one Indian myna bird, who would be responsible for running the joint.

SPONGE CAKE

3 eggs

½ cup/110 g castor sugar

¾ cup/95 g self-raising flour

¼ cup/30 g cornflour

15 g butter

3 tablespoons boiling water

CHOCOLATE ICING

3⅓ cups/500 g icing sugar
mixture

⅓ cup/35 g cocoa

15 g butter, softened

½ cup/125 ml milk

2 cups/190 g desiccated coconut

METHOD

Preheat the oven to 180°C/350°F/gas mark 4.

Line a 20 cm × 30 cm × 3 cm/8 in × 12 in × 1½ in lamington tin with baking paper.

In a large bowl, beat the eggs until light, then gradually add the sugar until the mixture is thick and mousse-like.

Sift the two flours together several times. Cube the butter and dissolve in the boiling water.

Sift the flours over the egg mixture and fold through carefully. Add the butter and water mixture and quickly fold through. Pour into the prepared lamington tin and bake for 30 minutes, or until the sponge is set when tested. Cool on a wire cake rack.

Leave the cake overnight before cutting. Trim the brown top and sides from the cake and cut into 16 cubes.

To make the icing, sift the icing sugar and cocoa together into a heatproof bowl. Add the butter and milk, stirring until thoroughly mixed. Place the bowl over hot water and stir until smooth and shiny.

Holding the cubes on a cake fork, dip each into the chocolate icing and let the excess drip off. Roll each in the coconut to coat evenly, stand on a wire cake rack to dry.

Makes 16

Lawrence of Arabia and the Bedouin's Cat Shoes

Of Sophia Shebaldin what is there to say? The top letter writer of them all seemed to have been written out. All the letters she wrote for Cleopatra's Cat must have cured her of letter writing forever. Perhaps, with all that had happened to her, just the mere act of writing a letter brought back too many painful memories. The news Mrs Moses received of her was second-hand, and scrappy at that. It came from the professor, who wasn't very good at gossip or remembering the things women wanted to know. He had accompanied Sophia Shebaldin to England and had also managed to find her a ginger kitten, the pick of a litter belonging to a ginger tabby, a long-time resident of

Magdalen College, Oxford. True to her word, Sophia christened it Sir Frederick Treves, purchased a cat basket at Liberty, and bought a second-class cabin ticket on a steamer bound for Port Said.

The first news of her continued existence came five years after the First World War when Colonel Lawrence of Arabia was interviewed by the BBC radio programme, *Traveller's Tales*. The interviewer, perhaps hoping to get the programme underway in a controversial way, remarked on the fact that Lawrence was wearing a curious looking pair of open sandals in the middle of an English winter.

Lawrence laughed. 'Oh, you mean my cat shoes.'

'Do you have a problem with your feet, Colonel Lawrence?' the BBC man inquired. 'Perhaps a legacy from fighting in the desert with the Bedouin tribesmen?'

'Good heavens no! In fact, entirely the opposite is the case,' Lawrence exclaimed. Then he told the story of how he had been presented with the sandals by an elder among the Bedouin. 'The sandals he gave me were quite different from the ubiquitous Egyptian toe sandal,' Lawrence explained, adding that his Bedouin host had called the sandals 'cat shoes' and it was obvious that they were held in high regard by the old Arab.

The sandals, more European than Arab in design, were curiously different in the construction of the sole. For instance, the upper side of the leather sole was built up on the inside of the instep so that the sandal seemed naturally to mould to the contour of the foot. Furthermore, the upper side of the sole, that is to say the surface upon which the foot rested, was covered with hundreds of little leather nodules. These nodules pressed into the sole of the foot with what was, initially, a decidedly uncomfortable result.

The old man had grinned knowingly when Lawrence, having slipped the sandals on, made a wry face as he attempted to walk. Lawrence knew he could not possibly reject the sandals for fear of insulting his host. So he was forced to persevere with the strange footwear through one long, very hot day.

That evening, in the privacy of his tent, he removed what he had come to think of in the course of the day as his torture sandals, worn in the name of Anglo–Arab relations. Yet he was suddenly aware that he'd quite forgotten about their existence from about mid-afternoon. Not only that, but his feet seemed much less tired than usual. The camel he had been riding that day had become lame and he had been obliged to walk a great distance across the hot sand. Now, curiously, his feet felt better than he could ever remember.

When the opportunity arose Lawrence asked his Bedouin host about the sandals, thinking them to be some ancient secret of Bedouin leather craft. Instead he was told that the sandals were made by a Russian woman who lived alone with a red cat on the edge of the small town of El Burumbul, some hundred and fifty miles from Cairo. The Bedouin elder then went on to tell Lawrence the curious tale of the origin of the cat shoes.

One day, several years previously, a young Bedouin goat-herd had badly sprained his ankle chasing a goat and was in such terrible pain that he was unable to walk. After dragging himself along for some distance he was finally overcome by the heat and lay helpless in the blistering midday sun. He was nowhere near the Bedouin camp and was also without water, having removed the goatskin gourd strung across his shoulders the better to chase the goat. Now, as he lay in a delirium, a strange white woman wearing a large straw hat emerged, seemingly out of nowhere. She lifted the young boy onto her back and carried him more than a mile to a small mud hovel, taking the urchin into the dark, cool interior of her home. She bathed his forehead until he became conscious and then began to work on his sprain. So effective was her treatment that by late evening, with the help of a stick, he was able to return to his camp.

The goats had returned at sunset on their own accord and the boy's family and other members of the tribe had immediately set out to look for him. They were hampered by a new moon but eventually they came upon his water bag, and judging from its contents they decided the lad had not taken water since about ten that morning. From this fact they concluded that if he was not dead by now he would be wandering in the desert quite delirious. They reluctantly returned, having given him up for lost. In fact the Bedouin women had already begun their keening, knowing that if he was not already dead the night, when the temperature often got down below freezing, would finish him off. Without water during the day, or the means to make a fire at night, the young goat boy would most certainly perish. In the morning they would watch the sky for circling vultures so that they might find his body to bury it. 'There was great rejoicing,' the old Arab said, 'when the boy entered the camp with the stars at the zenith.'

The following day the boy's father went to the woman's tiny house to thank her for his son's safe return and, as a token of his gratitude, he presented her with a small sack of dates and dried apricots. The woman, who had not covered her face at his approach and who seemed not to understand why he had come, at first refused the gift. But when he insisted, even showing some anger at her refusal, she changed her mind. Then, much to the man's embarrassment, she had neutralised his gift with a pair of curious-looking sandals, pressing them into his reluctant hands and then pointing to his feet.

Like Lawrence, the man could not refuse the white lady's gift without insulting her. He returned with them to the camp where he told of the red cat and the woman infidel who wore a great hat of plaited grass and dared to show her face to a male stranger.

Everyone shook their heads in dismay at this boldness, but then enjoyed a good laugh at the notion of wearing the ridiculous looking sandals. More in jest than anything else, the boy's father, hoping to enjoy the attention he had received a bit more, had worn the strange sandals for a few hours. Like Lawrence, he discovered that they possessed some sort of magic healing power.

To cut a long story short, all the Bedouin started wearing them. Soon the strange lady with her red cat had a small but thriving business going among the tribesmen.

The Bedouin elder spread his hands and gave Lawrence an almost toothless smile. 'That is the story of your sandals, Lourens *effendi*. We still get the cat shoes from this white woman with the red cat.'

Lawrence was aware of the ability of the Bedouin to fashion almost anything with their hands. 'But why do you not make them for yourselves?' he asked.

The elder looked shocked. 'You do not understand, Lourens, it is the red cat, the magic red cat. Have you seen how a cat walks, silent, perfectly balanced, as though on air? A cat's paws are always cool. It is the same with the cat shoes the woman makes, there is magic in them, a magic we dare not copy for fear of Allah's wrath that we should steal an idea from an infidel.'

Lawrence of Arabia then told the man from the BBC how he took the sandals back to England with him, where he wore them increasingly until the idea of wearing a sensible pair of English brogues became anathema to him. Slowly he had come to realise that what happened to your feet largely decided the degree of your general wellbeing. He said that his cat shoes proved to be almost indestructible and when the soles wore thin he simply had them resoled. Now the cat shoes were the footwear he preferred and, as often as not, he wore them with a collar and tie and his Sunday-best suit. The local people in the village in which he lived eventually came to accept the sandals as a sign of his growing eccentricity. That is, until a chance conversation occurred between himself and a visiting Swiss chiropodist.

It seemed a certain Dr Scholl had come to visit a neighbour and had been introduced to Lawrence. The foot doctor had noted Lawrence's sandals and questioned him about them. Lawrence had removed a sandal, or cat shoe as he called it, and handed it to the famous chiropodist, at the same time vouching for its efficacy.

The Swiss foot doctor had examined the shoe with great interest, rubbing his thumb up and down the hundreds of tiny leather nodules that covered the surface of the inner sole.

'It is so obvious!' he exclaimed in a surprised voice. 'So very obvious! Why did I not think myself of this?' He looked up at Lawrence. 'My dear Colonel Lawrence, are you aware that every nerve in the human body ends in the feet?' He ran his thumb over the myriad little nodules again. 'These sharp little bumps act as a constant massage, stimulating the blood flow through the feet and up into the body.' He returned the sandals to Colonel Lawrence and began to polish his glasses with a clean white handkerchief. '*Wunderbar!* Wonderful!' he repeated and his eyes positively shone. '*Ja!* We shall see what I can do with this idea! You are a genius, Colonel Lawrence!'

'Not me, my dear fellow, some Russian woman in the Arabian desert who lives with a ginger cat, she's your true genius.'

Sophia Shebaldin was never heard of again, but around the mid-1930s the Bedouin ceased wearing cat shoes. Mrs Moses always supposed that Sophia Shebaldin must have passed away around that time.

As for Dr Scholl, the chiropodist who had visited Lawrence? His is by now a well-known success story.

Of Sir Frederick Treves, the ginger cat, nothing is also known. But if you should visit the Pyramids in Gaza you will notice the presence of a great many cats which, since time out of mind, have been regarded by Egyptians as sacred animals. It is surprising how many of these creatures are distinctly ginger in colour.

The Mechanic and the Maid from the Astra Hotel

I have left the story of what happened to Mr Petrov of the beluga caviar fame until last, not because it is the most dramatic story of them all, but because it is the one that affects me the most.

As was always expected, Mr Petrov made a beeline for New York where he would meet his five sisters and his beloved Katya Markova of the scorpion sting.

But perhaps the scorpion had left some of its unfortunate nature behind in the poison it had injected into the slim and pretty ankle of Mr Petrov's proposed bride. Because, when he eventually arrived, he was met by his five sisters who had waited for seven hours outside the immigration shed on Ellis Island to welcome their brother to America. Of Katya Markova there was no sign.

Mr Petrov, always polite, held each of his loving sisters in his arms and amid copious tears they welcomed him to the land of the free. It was only after a long ride to the Lower East Side in a modern internal combustion motor called an omnibus that he asked about Katya Markova.

For some moments his sisters were silent, each reluctant to be the one to tell him, but then the eldest, Nadia, spoke. 'She met a banker named J.P. Morgan Jnr,' she said tentatively.

'So who is this Mr Morgan?' Mr Petrov asked, 'What has he done to Katya?'

'She is his mistress!' they all cried and then collectively burst into tears.

'Mistress? What is a mistress?'

'His fancy woman,' Nadia said quietly.

Mr Petrov could hardly believe his ears. 'But she is promised to me, we are betrothed!'

'This is America, my brother, the old rules do not apply here,' Nadia answered, averting her eyes from those of her brother.

'He is an old man of fifty years, he gave her a fur coat and a diamond ring!' Natasha, the youngest, exclaimed. 'She has also an automobile and a chauffeur and a nice brownstone house!'

'I will kill him, it is the only honourable thing to do!' Mr Petrov swore.

But Mr Petrov did no such thing. Instead he got a job on the waterfront in the fish markets. But he found that while life in America was good, he thought increasingly about Mrs Moses with whom he seemed to have formed such a good partnership on the road.

He also discovered that each of his sisters had a beau, as the Americans called it, a young man who sought their hand in marriage. They had all refrained from accepting the various proposals, waiting for their brother to arrive to give his permission and blessing to the match. Nadia, for instance, had waited nearly three years, much to the chagrin of the widower shopkeeper who was to be her intended.

Mr Petrov could find no fault in any of the suitors and agreed that each of his sisters had his permission to wed. After all, he told himself, in Russia, with the furore over his so-called affair with Katya Markova and the spoiled caviar, they would have remained spinsters forever. Here in America they could start new lives and have families of their own – that was what the land of hope and glory was all about.

Nadia, despite being the first to find a sweetheart, was the last to wed, attending first to the wedding arrangements of all of her sisters and seeing that they brought a small dowry with them. Each had a traditional wedding in the Russian Orthodox church in Styvesant and, although these were modest enough affairs, Mr Petrov had to work for three years to pay for the wedding feasts. Finally Nadia took the vows, though not before she told

Mr Petrov that she was prepared to give up her fiancé if he required her to look after him.

After five years in America and with all his wedding debts paid Mr Petrov was free to leave for Australia. But, almost on the eve of his departure, America entered the war and he was drafted into the United States Army. The army trained him as a motor mechanic and sent him to fight in France and Germany. He returned to America a minor hero, having been twice mentioned in despatches.

Back in New York after the war Mr Petrov tried to forget Mrs Moses and bought a small fish shop with a war veteran's grant. But he found he couldn't settle down. Finally, he admitted to himself that he must do something about the one thing that had been scratching away at his heart ever since he'd come from Russia. He sold the fish shop and had sufficient money for the boat trip to Australia and a handsome gold and sapphire engagement ring and two wedding rings, one female and the other male.

Three months later, at sunset, with the waves lapping on the white sand, he proposed to Mrs Moses while they were walking along Bondi Beach. My great-grandma accepted immediately, she had always loved Mr Petrov but had never dared to think that he might reciprocate her feelings.

There's a part on one of the tapes where she says, 'When Papa went on his knees in the wet sand and asked me to marry him, I thought, Oh my God, a wave will come in and wash him away and I'll think it's all in my imagination!

Because Mr Petrov wasn't Jewish they were married at the registry office in the city and Whacker O'Sullivan was called upon to be the best man and chief witness. Almost all the Irish and most of the permanent population of Bondi Beach came to the wedding, invited or not. A Russian–Irish–Australian wedding is no affair for the timid, and a grand time was had by all. Well after midnight, three local crims out on probation and the Mayor of Waverley carried Sergeant Bumper O'Flynn home in a deckchair used as a stretcher.

There were plenty of jobs for blacksmiths in Australia after the First World War but, from that very first ride in an omnibus in New York, Mr Petrov had fallen in love with the internal combustion engine. Besides, his war experience made him a very good motor mechanic. So, with the savings Mrs Moses had made working as a cook at the Astra Hotel, they bought a tin shed at the corner of Curlewis Street and Campbell Parade and turned it into a combination garage and smithy.

For several years they lived in two fibro rooms behind the garage and that was where my grandfather, who would one day work in the ABC on the *Country Hour* programme, was born. When he grew up he became captain of the Bondi Surf Life Saving Club and eventually married Whacker O'Sullivan's daughter, Maureen, who gave him three sons and a daughter, my little freckly mum.

Our family isn't rich. My father is a B.P. dealer and we live in

286

quite a nice house on the point overlooking Bondi Beach. Sometimes I stand on the rocks at Ben Buckler and look out to sea, knowing that there is no land between me all the way to South America, where the waves lapping at my feet have just come from.

The reason I do this is because I have a boyfriend from Argentina who is two years older than me. His real name is Jesus Navarro, but because this is Australia and you can't go around the place being called Jesus, he calls himself Jay. His older brother, Raoul, was a student revolutionary in a regional city called Cordoba and, like thousands of other students, disappeared at The Time of the Generals. His mother was one of the tens of thousands of women who were true gatherers and who wore the white scarf of silent vigil and carried pictures of their sons in the great women's gatherings that finally brought about the downfall of the military junta, those brutal hunters of the pampas who murdered their own sons and daughters.

Jay plays the Spanish guitar and sings wonderful mournful songs and he's nice. I mean he is *really* nice, not like Australian boys. But then I don't suppose he'll hang around until I've become a doctor and gone to Somalia.

Well, that's the story of my great-grandmother and I can't help thinking that there are millions of stories like this one. It worries me a lot when we turn back boat people who risk their lives for a new life in a safe land. Sailing all the way across the treacherous China Sea with pirates likely to board their little boat and kill them is probably even braver than walking across Russia. How could anyone have the heart to turn them back from our shores?

Australia wouldn't be what it is if we hadn't taken in migrants. In my school there is every kind of racial type you could imagine, and religions too. We have Christians, of course, but Muslims, Buddhists, Jews and Hindus as well. The really bright kids are usually either migrants or first-generation Australians who have parents who've had a hard time elsewhere and want their children to succeed. Their kids work terribly hard compared to Australians like Sue and me.

So, my theory that I am the sum total of every human ever born on this planet is not as weird as it sounds. Australia is one of the most polyglot nations on earth. We have the blood and the brains of just about everyone and we've managed to bring all these people here without religious or racial wars. Except, of course, when we first came, when we killed most of the Aboriginal people. Which can't be forgiven, ever. But even the indigenous people have now mixed their blood with everyone else who came to Australia. So, my theory still works. People can have different religions and come from different ethnic backgrounds and co-exist peacefully as one nation. All you have to do is watch out for the hunters and their hidden agendas and give the gatherers a chance.

Well, that's my theory, anyway, and I think the story of my great-grandmother and the Family Frying Pan proves it, don't you?

6 cloves garlic

2 tablespoons extra virgin
olive oil

1 × 2 kg/4½ lb leg of
lamb, trimmed of fat

salt and black pepper,
freshly ground

juice of a lemon

500 ml/16 fl oz natural
yoghurt

1 cup fresh mint,
finely chopped

lemon wedges

'BONDI OR THE BUSH' LAMB

METHOD

Halve the garlic cloves and dip them into some extra virgin olive oil.

Make 12 small cuts in the lamb and insert the garlic halves. Rub the lamb with salt and pepper and pour the lemon juice over it.

Combine the yoghurt and mint in a bowl, and spread over the lamb. Marinate in the refrigerator for several hours, preferably overnight.

Preheat the oven to 200°C/400°F/gas mark 6.

Wrap the lamb in foil and place in a baking dish. Bake in the preheated oven for 15 minutes, then reduce the heat to 180°C/350°F/gas mark 4 and cook for a further hour. Remove the foil and cook for a further 30 minutes for pink lamb. You will need to cook it for longer if you like it medium or well done.

Garnish with lemon wedges and serve with vegetables or a salad.

Serves 10